KT-379-292

The Open University

## K207 The Law and Social Work in Scotland

# Block Criminal Justice 3

Prepared for the course team by Elizabeth Stokes

Based on original material prepared for the course team
by Kathryn  Cameron, Janice West with Lesley-Anne Cull
and Jeremy Roche,  and updates by David Higginson,
Sarah Henderson and  Patricia McCulloch

The Social Work Degree Programme

The Open University
Walton Hall, Milton Keynes
MK7 6AA
First published 2007

Copyright © 2007 The Open University

All rights reserved. No part of this publication may be reproduced, stored in a retrieval system, transmitted or utilised in any form or by any means, electronic, mechanical, photocopying, recording or otherwise, without written permission from the publisher or a licence from the Copyright Licensing Agency Ltd. Details of such licences (for reprographic reproduction) may be obtained from the Copyright Licensing Agency Ltd, Saffron House, 6–10 Kirby Street, London EC1N 8TS; website www.cla.co.uk/.

Open University course materials may also be made available in electronic formats for use by students of the University. All rights, including copyright and related rights and database rights, in electronic course materials and their contents are owned by or licensed to The Open University, or otherwise used by The Open University as permitted by applicable law.

In using electronic course materials and their contents you agree that your use will be solely for the purposes of following an Open University course of study or otherwise as licensed by The Open University or its assigns.

Except as permitted above you undertake not to copy, store in any medium (including electronic storage or use in a website), distribute, transmit or retransmit, broadcast, modify or show in public such electronic materials in whole or in part without the prior written consent of The Open University or in accordance with the Copyright, Designs and Patents Act 1988.

Edited and designed by The Open University

Typeset in India by Alden Prepress Services, Chennai

Printed and bound in the United Kingdom by Cambrian Printers, Aberystwyth SY23 3TN

ISBN 978 0 7492 1941 3

1.1

The paper used in this publication contains pulp sourced from forests independently certified to the Forest Stewardship Council (FSC) principles and criteria.
Chain of custody certification allows the pulp from these forests to be tracked to the end use. (see www.fsc-uk.org).

# Contents

# Introduction

## Aims

- To introduce you to the meaning of criminal justice.
- To outline the adult criminal justice process in Scotland and its institutions.
- To provide an understanding of the legal framework for social work practice in the criminal justice process.
- To consider the position of children and young people who offend.
- To consider the position of mentally disordered people within the criminal justice process.
- To identify the knowledge, skills and values required for effective criminal justice social work practice.
- To encourage reflection on how social work values can be promoted in criminal justice settings.
- To situate criminal justice practice within a broader policy context.
- To help students to understand the complex relationships between justice care and control and the practical and ethical effects of these.

This block examines the different social work roles and responsibilities in the criminal justice process and in work with children and young people who offend. You will be introduced to the legal frameworks that shape practice and the key knowledge, skills and values that should inform and assist effective and ethical social work in this area.

Block 3 is divided into four sections:

1   Crime, justice and social work
2   Social work in the criminal justice process
3   Children, young people and criminal justice
4   Mental disorder and criminal justice.

An understanding of the law is fundamental to social work practice in criminal justice and youth justice settings. The criminal law is one of the most powerful instruments of social control and the sanctions that are available to the criminal courts have the potential to impose restrictions on the liberty of individuals. Social workers in this area have a responsibility towards the general public and the courts to protect the public and ensure their wellbeing. At the same time they have obligations towards those who are caught up in the criminal justice process, who may be vulnerable and in need of social work services. The challenges posed by the often complex relationships between justice, care and control in this area will therefore be explored throughout this block.

The first section will provide you with the opportunity to reflect on the meaning of criminal justice and the demands that are placed on social work in this context. It will also allow you to consider the relevance of social work values to practice in the criminal justice process before you encounter the detail of the legal frameworks in the sections that follow.

Section 2 outlines the adult criminal justice process and the roles and responsibilities of criminal justice social work services. Key practice skills such as risk assessment and the management of offenders in the community are considered within this legal framework and the importance of the social work role is explored.

Section 3 covers the role of social workers in youth justice teams and the position of children and young people who offend. An understanding of this topic requires familiarity with two sometimes conflicting legal frameworks and different areas of social work practice.

Finally, Section 4 looks at the position of people who are mentally disordered and come into contact with the criminal justice process. This topic raises questions of vulnerability and risk that have clear implications for criminal justice social work. It also involves the consideration of a third legal framework, governed by mental health legislation, and the intersections between criminal justice and mental health disposals.

You will notice that this block is illustrated with flow charts and diagrams to help you to make sense of the stages in the decision-making process and the options available in individual cases. You may find it useful to make a separate copy of these to enable easy reference throughout your studies. Electronic copies can be accessed via the course website.

# 1 Crime, justice and social work

For this section you need:

- audio CD
- course website access for online activities
- Reader, Chapter 9.

## Core questions

- What is criminal justice?
- Why do social workers need to know about the criminal justice process?
- What is the social work role in the criminal justice process?
- How do policy changes impact on this role?
- Which legislation and guidance provides the framework for criminal justice social work services?
- How might the dual role of the social worker create tensions for social work practice in the criminal justice process?

## 1.1 Introduction

Over the last two decades crime and its control have become clear concerns for politicians, communities and victims of crime. In the same period social work's role in the criminal justice process has become more pronounced and, many would argue, more complex. The first section of this block therefore aims to introduce you to this background, against which the social work role in criminal justice can be more readily understood.

In this highly charged area of social work practice, it is essential that social workers understand the legal frameworks that govern criminal justice social work. However, it is also important to recognise that the law, and social work decision makers, do not operate in a vacuum. Law is subject to change, particularly in this setting, as 'criminal justice policy is more liable to sudden, politically motivated changes of direction than is social policy in other fields' (Smith, 2002, p. 309). The requirements of the legal framework can therefore only really be understood within the wider social, cultural and historical contexts that impact on policy, legislation and practice.

We will see in this section that a range of competing demands are made of the criminal justice process and its institutions, which inevitably creates tensions and dilemmas for practitioners. You will be asked to reflect on how these might affect social work practice, and to consider how a commitment to social work values and a more critical appreciation of the law might aid decision making in this area.

We will start by taking a closer look at the meaning of criminal justice.

## 1.2 What is criminal justice?

Our familiarity with criminal justice is both a benefit and a blight. ... The familiarity fed by [a] daily diet of criminal justice stories (fact and fictional) has certain advantages. We share a basic perception of what the police do, what a courtroom looks like, and what happens inside the prison walls. But familiarity has its dangers also. We may be less inclined to question the very existence of the criminal justice system and the power it wields over us.

(Zedner, 2004, p. 1)

In contrast to other areas of law (which often fall outside of public consciousness) the idea of criminal justice is instantly familiar. Criminal justice is the legal system's response to crime and involves a process of investigation, prosecution, conviction and punishment. It is perhaps the most public face of the Scottish legal system: the institutions of criminal justice are more visible than their civil counterparts and have entered into popular culture as we are entertained by the drama of crime and attempts to control it. Criminal justice has also become a central part of political life. The workings of this part of the legal system are subject to close scrutiny and often found wanting. In fact, 'since devolution virtually every aspect of criminal justice has been subject to consultation, review and legislation' (Croall, 2006, p. 587).

It is not surprising therefore that there is a high level of interest in crime and justice; almost everyone has a view about crime and its control. Activity 1 provides you with an opportunity to think about public attitudes to criminal justice issues and to consider what shapes your own opinions in this area.

---

Allow about 20 minutes   ## Activity 1   Exploring public attitudes to crime and its control

Box 1 contains a number of statements about crime drawn from recent political debates, media reports and public comment. Make notes outlining your response to each statement and think about how often you have heard similar views expressed (in the media and/or in conversation with family members, friends or colleagues).

How do these statements compare with your own views?

What do they tell us about public attitudes to crime and its control?

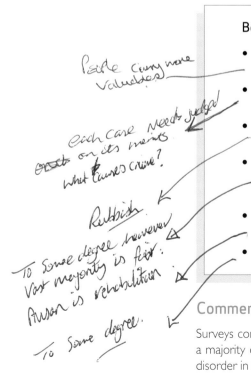

### Box 1   Examples of current views on crime

- The streets are more violent nowadays; I'm afraid to go out at night. — More exposure through media - More cases of stealing - eg mobile Phones
- We need to be tough on crime and tough on the causes of crime.
- Young people today have no respect; they hang around in gangs and terrorise neighbourhoods.
- It is time to redress the balance in favour of the victims of crime and ordinary decent families who deserve a better quality of life in their own homes.
- What we need is proper punishment instead of these holiday camps they get sent to.
- I blame the parents.

*Handwritten annotations in margin: People carry more valuables? Each case needs judged on its merits — what causes crime? Rubbish. To some degree however. Vast majority is fair. Prison is rehabilitation. To some degree. To*

### Comment

Surveys conducted into attitudes to crime and criminal justice consistently show that a majority of the general public are very concerned about the problems of crime and disorder in society and are critical of the legal system's response (Anderson et al., 2002;

Hutton, 2005). Government policy has reflected these concerns and promised tough measures in an attempt to tackle crime more effectively, to restore confidence in criminal justice and allay public fears. The statements above were selected to represent these popular views and should already be familiar to you, whether or not you agree with their sentiments.

Your response to these statements will inevitably be shaped by your experience of crime and the criminal justice system, and may also be informed by media representations of criminal justice issues (fact and fictional). Research studies have demonstrated that there is a lack of public knowledge about crime and the criminal justice system and some common misconceptions about both. For example, there is a widespread perception that crime is on the increase and has become more violent and random in character over the past decade. This perception may reflect the tendency of the media to select and dramatise sensational crime stories, but it is not supported by statistical accounts, which show overall crime levels falling in the same period. While violent crime levels have been increasing they still make up only a small proportion of recorded offences (around 6 per cent). There is also a common perception that sentencing is too lenient, but when asked to participate in a sentencing exercise and provided with more information about a particular offence, focus groups suggest sentences that are broadly in line with current sentencing practice (Anderson et al., 2002; Hutton, 2005).

The existence of a gap between public perceptions and actual practice is an important finding when you recall that public opinion continues to affect the direction of criminal justice policy. If you look again at the language used in these statements to describe crime and those who offend, you will see concern reflected about crime control, public safety and leniency. The tone of public comment is often punitive (tough) and moralistic, with a clear distinction being made between offenders ('they/them') and 'ordinary decent' members of the public ('we/us'), who are their potential victims. It is important to remember that social work with offenders takes place within this environment and is inevitably influenced and constrained by these views.

When you consider the current climate of opinion, the quotation at the beginning of this section is more easily understood. Zedner warns readers to look beyond their initial assumptions about criminal justice, to question its purpose and be open to different interpretations. She reminds us that the criminal justice system is a powerful instrument in which legal actors such as the police, prosecutors and the judiciary make decisions affecting people's lives and liberty, wielding power over all of us.

Activity 2 asks you to think again about who the criminal justice system focuses upon.

Allow about 20 minutes

## Activity 2   Who is a criminal?

Spend a few minutes making notes to describe what or who you think of when talking about 'criminals' or 'offenders'. Then answer the following questions.

Who is a criminal?

1   A person who commits a criminal act?

2   A person who is suspected of a crime?

3   A person who is convicted of a crime?

4   Someone who will commit a crime in the future?

5   A bad or evil person?

6     A violent, dangerous or persistent offender? ✓

7     Someone not like 'us'? ✓

8     You or I? ✓

## Comment

This activity should have alerted you to some of the difficulties with the label 'criminal', a word which is loaded with censure and has stigmatising effects. Part of the function of the criminal justice system is to determine whether a person has committed a criminal act and can be labelled an 'offender'. For this reason 'suspects' and 'the accused' retain greater rights than an offender. They are presumed innocent until proven otherwise. In the absence of a confession a court must decide whether the accused has committed the act alleged, with a guilty mind, and without a legitimate defence. In this way the criminal justice system helps to construct who is (and is not) a criminal and aims to do justice in a particular case. But miscarriages of justice can happen. The legal system is reliant on evidence from witnesses and human decision makers, who are fallible and can also be influenced by social prejudice and preconceptions about who is, or should be to blame.

This picture is further complicated by the commonplace assertion that not all actual offenders are 'real criminals', because of the ambivalence with which certain offences are viewed. What, for example, do you make of people who drive above the speed limit, ignore the smoking ban, or clip their children around the ear? All are crimes in Scotland, but does that make the actor a criminal? The changing social context also means that the definition of who is a criminal shifts over time. For example not wearing a seatbelt or using a mobile phone whilst driving are now offences, but were not previously.

As we saw in the last activity there is a tendency to exclude the criminal from our realm and see them as someone other than ourselves. It is easy to fall into the trap of assuming that the force of the criminal justice system can only be used against others, and therefore to lack concern about the legal safeguards that are a necessary part of its role. Research from self-report studies, however, suggests that offending behaviour is far more widespread than official crime statistics indicate, and, for young males at least, is relatively 'normal'. The them/us categorisation is therefore difficult to sustain. Nor is it appropriate to see offenders and victims as mutually exclusive labels. It is, of course, possible to be both.

Care should be taken in the language used to describe those who are drawn in to the criminal justice process. It is important to remember that the subjects of criminal justice are people first and legal categories second. The attribution of labels can obscure this.

By now you will be beginning to appreciate that there is no straightforward answer to the question 'What is criminal justice?' There is obviously room for disagreement about what should be 'criminal' and what constitutes 'justice' and these debates will continue to influence the workings of the legal system that is designed to achieve it.

In the opening quote of this section Zedner suggests that we should question the very existence of the criminal justice system, and ask why we choose to respond to crime in this way. This assertion may seem quite strange if you assume that the only possible response to crime is law enforcement and punishment. Activity 3 is designed to demonstrate that the criminal justice system is in reality limited in its ability to control crime through punishment, and has a number of other aims.

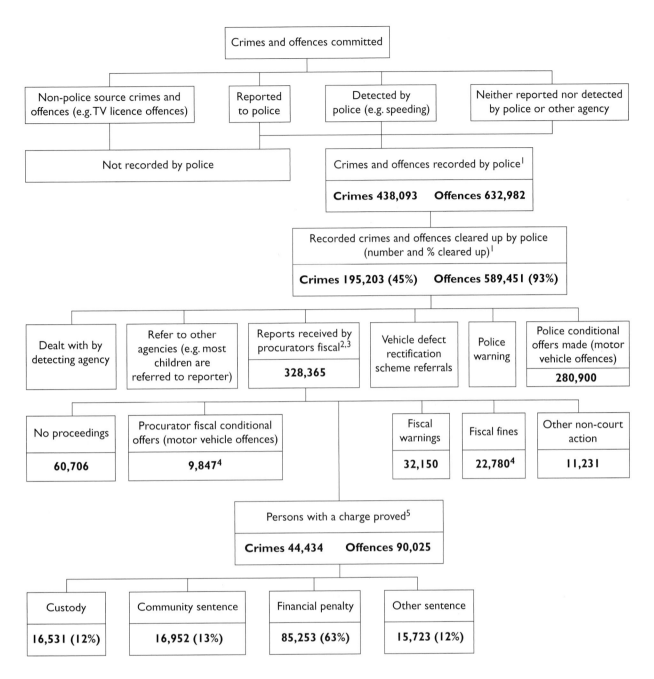

Figure 1 contains the following flow diagram:

**Crimes and offences committed**

- Non-police source crimes and offences (e.g. TV licence offences)
- Reported to police
- Detected by police (e.g. speeding)
- Neither reported nor detected by police or other agency

**Not recorded by police**

**Crimes and offences recorded by police[1]**

**Crimes 438,093     Offences 632,982**

**Recorded crimes and offences cleared up by police (number and % cleared up)[1]**

**Crimes 195,203 (45%)     Offences 589,451 (93%)**

- Dealt with by detecting agency
- Refer to other agencies (e.g. most children are referred to reporter)
- Reports received by procurators fiscal[2,3]

  **328,365**
- Vehicle defect rectification scheme referrals
- Police warning
- Police conditional offers made (motor vehicle offences)

  **280,900**

- No proceedings

  **60,706**
- Procurator fiscal conditional offers (motor vehicle offences)

  **9,847[4]**
- Fiscal warnings

  **32,150**
- Fiscal fines

  **22,780[4]**
- Other non-court action

  **11,231**

**Persons with a charge proved[5]**

**Crimes 44,434     Offences 90,025**

- Custody

  **16,531 (12%)**
- Community sentence

  **16,952 (13%)**
- Financial penalty

  **85,253 (63%)**
- Other sentence

  **15,723 (12%)**

1  Crimes recorded in 2004/05 may not be cleared up or dealt with until 2005/06 or later.
2  A report to the procurator fiscal may involve more than one crime or offence and more than one alleged offender.
3  The total number of reports to the fiscal includes reports on non-criminal matters such as sudden deaths.
4  Figures relate to offers which were accepted.
5  Figures for persons with a charge proved count the number of occasions on which a person is convicted.

A number of outcomes may result in subsequent prosecutions or referrals to other agencies, for example if a condition such as payment of a fixed penalty is not complied with. For simplicity, these pathways are not shown in the diagram.

Figure 1    Overview of action within the criminal justice system 2004/5 (Scottish Executive, 2006a, p. 7)

Allow about 30 minutes    ## Activity 3    Choice and the criminal justice process

Figure 1 contains a flow diagram of actions taken in the criminal justice process from the commission of crime to the attribution of punishment. (For recording purposes only, the statistics on the diagram divide breaches of the criminal law into 'crimes' and 'offences'. This is in order to reflect the relative seriousness of the acts involved. 'Crimes' are considered more serious than 'offences' but this practice has no basis in law.) Read the statistics on the diagram and then write notes in answer to the following questions:

*No*  1    Do all crimes and offences committed end up in the criminal justice process?

2    Do all crimes and offences recorded by the police get cleared up (i.e. where a suspect is identified and there is sufficient evidence to justify the consideration of criminal proceedings)?

3    Do all of the cases received by prosecutors (the procurators fiscal) result in a court hearing?

4    Do all prosecutions result in conviction?

5    What does this diagram tell you about the criminal justice process?

## Comment

If the Scottish criminal justice process is to be judged on the basis of its ability to ensure that offenders are convicted and punished for their crimes then the statistics given in Figure 1 above indicate that it is not very effective. In 2004/05 less than 13 per cent of the crimes and offences recorded by the police ended in a conviction. The vast majority of criminal offences never reach this stage. In 2003 the Scottish Crime Survey estimated that less than a quarter of the offences that it identified were recorded by the police; many are neither reported nor detected and remain untouched by the process of criminal justice.

It would be wrong, however, to interpret these figures as a failure of the 'system' to address the crime problem. There are many reasons for the attrition in the number of offences that reach the end point of the criminal justice process (the sentencing stage). The police for example are heavily reliant on the public to bring 'crimes' to their attention, but we may not be aware that we are 'victims', or may not choose to report an offence for a variety of reasons that have nothing to do with the effectiveness of the police. In those that are reported it may not be possible to identify an offender, or the allegations may be found to be false, or there may not be sufficient evidence to proceed with a prosecution, and so on. The capacity of law enforcement is therefore limited by the social context in which it operates. Attitudes to crime, and perceptions of who or what is 'criminal', influence the intake of the criminal justice process and which cases progress to each stage.

From a different perspective the reduction in cases from police investigation to conviction could be interpreted as a success, an indication that the safeguards in the legal process designed to protect innocents are working. The police, procurators fiscal and the courts all have a role to secure safe convictions and filter out cases that cannot be proved to the high standard required (beyond reasonable doubt).

You should also have noted that other options are available to the various decision makers at each stage. Cases can be diverted out of the criminal justice process by, for example, referral to other agencies or the issue of a warning. These diversions from prosecution and punishment are for the purpose of achieving other aims, such as earlier intervention, the assessment and treatment of needs and the avoidance of costly court proceedings. They do not fit the crime–punishment logic of criminal justice and show that alternative ideas exist about the best way to control crime. Practical pressures such as the cost of criminal justice are also taken into account.

All of these choices are structured by a legal framework: the law defines what is a crime, the rules of evidence and criminal procedure. But a wide degree of discretion is given to the legal actors involved, both at the institutional level (in the setting of aims, budgets and priorities) and to individual decision makers (who require flexibility to adapt to the needs of different cases). In this way the criminal justice process is far from systematic. What happens at one point in the system may have a knock-on effect on another, but they operate independently, have different functions and some conflicting aims. For example social

*[handwritten: → Good for TOLA?]*

workers, the police and the judiciary have very different professional roles and agendas. Their values and beliefs are shaped by their occupational training and cultures and do not always coincide. This can make working within the system difficult in the absence of a shared understanding of common aims and participants' roles.

*[handwritten: unlike (CSA9S)]*

There is currently no overarching statement of aims or objectives for the criminal justice system in Scotland, although concern over the need for its component parts to work together more effectively prompted a review by the Scottish Executive which suggested the framework for consultation in Box 2.

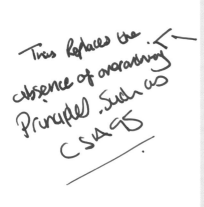

*[handwritten: This Replaces the absence of overarching Principles. Such as CSA 9S]*

---

**Box 2   Recommendations for criminal justice system objectives in Scotland**

*Aims:*

- To improve the safety and the feeling of safety of the people of Scotland and to deliver justice fairly and effectively

*Objectives:*

- To reduce the level of crime, disorder and offending
- To improve people's feeling of safety and the confidence of the whole community in the criminal justice system
- To improve the treatment of victims and witnesses
- To protect the rights of accused
- To improve efficiency and deal with cases with appropriate speed

*Values:*

- Integrity
- Fairness and impartiality
- Equality of treatment and respect for diversity

(Normand, 2003, part V)

---

As a broad summary of aims these recommendations clearly demonstrate that there are a number of demands made of the criminal justice process and its institutions which are not easy to reconcile in practice. We have already seen that there can be a tension between the objectives of crime control (where detection, prosecution, conviction and punishment are prioritised) and due process of law (the safeguards required to protect suspects, the accused and offenders from the power of criminal justice institutions). These aims are further complicated by the need to consider the perceptions of the public, victims and witnesses, and system management concerns for efficiency within the process. Criminal justice social workers have to negotiate these tensions, which help to explain the complexity of the social work task.

The limitations of criminal justice as a crime control measure were also recognised by the Normand Report. It noted that the formal legal system can play only a part in this as 'achievement of these objectives is dependent on other policies and other agencies' (Normand, 2003, para. 9.9). Local authorities, for example, have a role in the reduction of antisocial behaviour, the promotion of crime prevention and community safety strategies that require the engagement of their housing, education and social service functions. Government economic, social and legal policies also impact on crime and could even be said to create crime through the identification of new social harms and the introduction of new offences, such as those related to antisocial behaviour. Public expectations of the criminal justice process can seem unrealistic when set in this context.

The reduction in crime, disorder and offending remains a primary objective of criminal justice, but it is important to remember that this does not necessarily require the imposition of 'punishment' in the popular sense of the word. In the criminal justice process there are a range of sentences and disposals that reflect different ideas about how to reduce future offending, for example by attending to a person's rehabilitation needs or the use of victim–offender mediation to aid restorative justice. Diversion from prosecution and punishment is also an option in some cases, to avoid the potentially damaging effects of further involvement in the criminal justice and penal (or punishment) process. You will see in Sections 3 and 4 of this block that young offenders and the mentally disordered may be diverted, in order to avoid the exclusionary effects of being drawn into a system which can actually increase the chances of further offending. From this perspective Zedner's suggestion that the pursuit of criminal justice may not be the only appropriate response to crime is easier to comprehend. It is this belief that informs the distinctive Scottish approach to youth crime, which removes most children and young people from the criminal justice process to the welfare-oriented children's hearings system.

Both the law and practice in criminal justice is therefore informed by knowledge from the disciplines of criminology and penology about how best to respond to crime. The choices available to criminal justice actors are governed by law, but professional decision making requires an understanding of the causes of crime and the effects of punishment, which go beyond the remit of this course. This introductory section should, however, have alerted you to the fact that this knowledge is not value free. It is affected by personal attitudes and social, cultural and political perceptions about what constitutes crime and justice.

The next section considers the relevance of criminal justice to social work practice and how policy changes have affected this role.

## 1.3 Understanding the social work role

Social work often involves working with marginalised and disadvantaged populations who are vulnerable to crime and susceptible to criminalisation. All social workers can therefore benefit from an understanding of criminal justice as in the course of their work with service users, carers and their families, they will encounter people accused of criminal offences, witnesses and victims of crime who may be in need of advice and support.

However, the social work role in criminal justice extends beyond these incidental contacts. Many social workers do work that is directly related to the criminal justice system because their practice is with victims (e.g. victim support, rape crisis, domestic violence) or offenders (e.g. in bail hostels or providing programmes for offenders). Local authorities in Scotland in particular have statutory responsibility to provide criminal justice social work services to support the workings of

the criminal justice process through the assessment of individuals caught up in the system, the provision of information to the courts, and the supervision of offenders.

Social work therefore has a central role within the criminal justice process in Scotland, which can be contrasted to the position in England and Wales where probation work with adult offenders is commissioned by the National Offender Management Service (NOMS), separated from local authority control and social work functions. This reflects a difference of approach between the two jurisdictions in their choices about how best to respond to crime. Scottish criminal justice has traditionally adopted a more welfare-oriented approach, shaped by its distinctive legal culture and political history (McAra, 2005). An understanding of this penal context helps to explain the changing influences on the social work role in this area that continue to affect criminal justice social work practice today.

### The policy context

In 1968 'probation' or offender services became the responsibility of local authority social work departments, who were tasked with a general duty to 'promote social welfare' in their locality (section 12, Social Work (Scotland) Act 1968). This development was informed by the philosophy of the Kilbrandon Committee (Kilbrandon, 1964), which was appointed to consider the appropriate response to the increasing problem of juvenile crime. The Kilbrandon Report suggested a radical restructuring of children's services around the needs of children and families, in the belief that children who offend should not be differentiated from children in need of care and protection. Meeting the 'needs' of children in trouble was considered to be the best way of addressing their 'deeds', avoiding the possibly negative effects of a criminal justice response. Kilbrandon also advocated diversion and early voluntary intervention as forms of crime prevention, and the grouping of the full range of social work services for adults and children within one all-purpose department to better enable an appropriate response to complex social problems.

The merging of work with adult offenders within a generic social work service was significant because it clearly identified work with offenders as having a central welfare component, albeit with a level of control. At the heart of criminal justice social work, therefore, is the idea that supervision, control and assistance are provided to the offender as an 'alternative to punishment'. The Kilbrandon philosophy itself was influenced by the penal trends of the time, which showed a commitment to the rehabilitation and treatment of offenders and an awareness of the social causes of crime (agendas which continue to be strong in the minds of practitioners today).

Since the 1980s, however, criminal justice in Scotland has undergone major legislative and policy change. Social work has retained its key role and is now involved at almost every stage in the criminal justice process, but the ideological climate in which social work delivers key services has changed significantly and has been heavily influenced by the punishment-led rhetoric of successive governments. As the prison population in Scotland began to increase during this period, concerns were raised that criminal justice social work was not being given significant priority among the other social work tasks. The delivery of services to adult offenders was found to be patchy and there was a lack of judicial confidence in community disposals such as probation.

In 1988 a 'new' policy direction was outlined for Scotland by Malcolm Rifkind, then secretary of state for Scotland. This statement was reproduced in the *National Objectives and Standards for Social Work Services in the Criminal Justice System* in 1991 and still underpins Scottish policy and practice for criminal justice services today:

> There will always be those who commit serious or violent crimes and who pose a threat to society which requires them to be confined for significant periods. Nevertheless there are many good reasons for wishing to ensure that, as a society, we use prisons as sparingly as possible. While the use of imprisonment may be inescapable when dealing with violent offenders and those who commit the most serious crimes, we must question to what extent short sentences of imprisonment and periods of custody for fine default are an appropriate means of dealing with offenders and there is no single answer to that. Prisons are both expensive to build and run and do not provide the ideal environment in which to teach an offender to live a normal and law-abiding life, to work at a job or to maintain a family. If offenders can remain in the community, under suitable conditions, they should be able to maintain their family ties, opportunities for work or training and they may be better placed to make some reparation for their offence.
>
> (Rifkind, 1989, p. 85)

Activity 4 helps you to identify the key elements of this policy.

---

Allow about 15 minutes

## Activity 4    Understanding the twin-track approach

Reread the extract from the speech by Malcolm Rifkind above and make notes on what you consider to be the key messages in it about how best to respond to offending behaviour and the role of criminal justice social work. You may find it helpful to underline words or phrases which seem important.

Would you characterise his approach as **welfare oriented** and/or **punishment focused**? What do you think he believes the aims of punishment should be?

## Comment

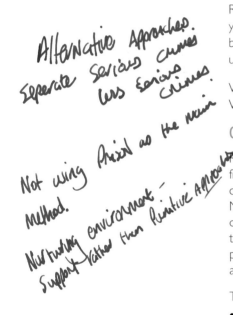

Rifkind's policy statement represents a shift in emphasis for criminal justice social work from providing services *for offenders* to providing services *to protect the public*. A clear distinction is made between violent and non-violent offenders for this reason. Nevertheless, in keeping with the Kilbrandon philosophy this policy also outlines a clear commitment to using prison sparingly and maintains a focus on reintegration and help that, it is argued, is unlikely to occur within a prison environment. It is not therefore possible to separate welfare and punishment; there are tensions between these two aims but they can also coexist within the penal process.

The key objectives can be summarised as follows:

- an overarching aim of *public protection*
- implementation of a *twin-track approach* in order to effectively and appropriately target disposals:

    All non-violent offenders, except the most serious, should be dealt with in the community.

    All violent offenders, except the less serious, may face custody as a means of protecting the public.

- a commitment to the *reduction in the unnecessary use of custody* through the development and delivery of effective community-based disposals.

Concerns for improved public protection and effectiveness in community disposals marked the beginning of a new era of managerialism for criminal justice social work. In 1991, 100 per cent central government funding was introduced for social work services to the criminal justice system, and the National Objectives and Standards for Social Work Services in the Criminal Justice System were published, setting out the core objectives, services to be provided and detailed guidance on their delivery (Social Work Services Group, 1991). These new structural arrangements both affirmed the importance of the social work role in this area and placed new demands on its performance, demonstrating the strength of the government's commitment to see social work deliver on this role.

These arrangements and the policy priorities outlined by Rifkind have largely survived the changes in political administration since the 1990s, a period which in England and Wales saw the social work qualification for work with adult offenders replaced and a hardening of attitudes towards offenders. Scotland has largely been insulated from these changes, although some commentators suggest that devolution has caused a 'sudden and dramatic politicisation' of criminal justice issues that threatens to undermine the welfarist tradition (McNeill and Batchelor, 2004; Croall, 2005). Nevertheless, recent statements contained in the consultation exercise *Re:duce, Re:habilitate, Re:form* (Scottish Executive, 2004a) and the resulting *Supporting Safer, Stronger Communities: Scotland's Criminal Justice Plan* (Scottish Executive, 2004b) show some continuity in policy concerns to reduce the rising numbers in Scottish prisons, to reduce reoffending rates through the delivery of effective community-based disposals and (albeit less vocally) to promote the social inclusion and rehabilitation of offenders. These at times conflicting objectives capture both the challenge and the opportunity facing social workers in the current policy context.

## The legal framework

> There are many competing pressures to direct the service in ways that may not be consistent with social work principles towards greater penal and correctional models. It is therefore essential to have a clear understanding of the policy and legal framework that creates the remit and legitimacy for the operation of social work in the criminal justice process.
>
> (Whyte, 2001, p. 7)

Whyte argues that an understanding of the legal framework is essential for social workers to appreciate the scope and limitations of their mandate. Box 3 contains a summary of the most important sources of law in this area.

---

### Box 3   The mandate for criminal justice social work

Social Work Scotland Act 1968 (as amended):

  section 12 – general duty on local authorities to 'promote social welfare' and power to provide the facilities they consider suitable in this task

  section 27 – provisions outlining the duty to provide criminal justice services (e.g. social background reports, supervision and care of offenders on court order or licence) and the funding of these services

National Objectives and Standards for Social Work Services in the
Criminal Justice System 1991 (as amended) – policy guidance
Management of Offenders etc. (Scotland) Act 2005 –
organisational structures and accountability.

The basic legal framework outlining the powers and duties of criminal
justice social work can be found in the Social Work Scotland Act 1968
(as amended). Section 27 of this Act outlines the specific services
that must be delivered by the local authority in receipt of central
government funding, but it does not explain the objectives of these
services or provide guidance on their exercise. Section 12 gives local
authorities the discretion to provide additional criminal justice services
(e.g. to victims) as part of their general responsibility to 'promote social
welfare'. These services, however, must compete with the whole
range of social work functions for local authority funds. The statutory
framework for criminal justice social work is therefore adaptable to
changes of direction in criminal justice policy and to different
interpretations of the social work role.

Detailed **policy guidance** is found in the **National Objectives and
Standards for Social Work Services in the Criminal Justice System
(NOS) (Scottish Executive, 2004c)**. These are not strictly a source of law
as they are **updated by the Scottish Executive**, but compliance with
these standards is supported by the **legal frameworks for social work
accountability**. Criminal justice services are inspected against these
requirements by the Social Work Inspection Agency (SWIA) (www),
and service planning and delivery must also meet the objectives of
executive guidance (s. 3(5) **Management of Offenders etc. (Scotland)
Act 2005, s. 5 Social Work (Scotland) Act 1968)**. Activity 5 helps you to
locate this important guidance and consider the scope of social work in
the criminal justice system.

---

Allow about 30 minutes

## Activity 5   National Objectives and Standards for Social Work Services in the Criminal Justice System

Website

Following the link from this activity on the course website, locate the NOS on the
Scottish Executive Criminal Justice Social Work pages. You will find it useful to
bookmark this link for future use. Click on the link to the first document – General
Issues – and read Chapters 1 and 2, making notes in answer to the following questions:

1   What policy goals does the government aim to achieve through the NOS?

2   What components should a comprehensive social work service in the criminal
    justice system include?

3   Which of these services attract 100 per cent funding from central government?

4   What are the functions of the NOS?

## Comment

You may have noticed that the stated components of a comprehensive social work
service in the criminal justice system (para. 8) go beyond the provision of centrally
funded services (para. 9). The detailed guidance in the NOS documents should not
therefore be mistaken for a comprehensive statement of what criminal justice social
work services must do. Mechanistic adherence to the requirements of these standards,
without recognising that discretion exists to provide additional services in line with

the wider objectives of criminal justice social work, would be an example of poor professional practice and does not fully explore the potential of the social work mandate.

A core function of the NOS is quality assurance to promote consistency in service provision across local areas and to enhance the confidence of the courts, the police and the public at large in community-based disposals. You should recall from Activity 1 that perceptions of leniency continue to challenge the legitimacy of these disposals, so the standards can also be interpreted as an attempt to impose more stringent requirements on social work with offenders, for example in relation to risk assessment and supervision. These are not, however, incompatible with a professional and effective social work role.

This can be seen from the overall policy objectives (paras 5 and 6), which are to reduce the use of custody, reduce the risk of reoffending and assist resettlement and social integration.

---

These objectives were updated in *Criminal Justice Social Work Services: National Priorities for 2001–2 and Onwards* (Justice Department, 2001), which reordered their priority as follows:

1  To make a contribution to increased community safety and public protection.

2  To reduce the use of unnecessary custody by providing effective community disposals.

3  To promote the social inclusion of offenders through rehabilitation, so reducing the level of offending.
(Justice Department (2001), p. 3, quoted in McNeill et al., 2005)

The change in order and language here is significant, and was usefully depicted in the 21st Century Social Work Review report *Reducing Reoffending: Key Priorities and Skills* (McNeill et al., 2005) as a triangle of interdependent outcomes.

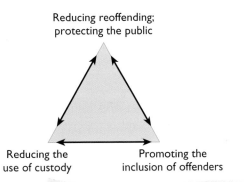

Reducing reoffending; protecting the public

Reducing the use of custody

Promoting the inclusion of offenders

Figure 2   The interdependence of the intended outcomes of criminal justice social work (McNeill et al., 2005, p. 8)

As Figure 2 illustrates, protecting the public (by reducing offending) is now at the apex of the triangle. Social work with offenders should first and foremost address offending behaviour and seek a reduction in that behaviour, but it is important to remember that this objective is shared with other criminal justice agencies such as the police and prisons. When viewed in this way it is clear that there may be tensions between public protection and the other aims, but McNeill et al. argue (and Scottish policy and practice recognise) that this primary objective cannot be achieved without effective community disposals, reducing the use of custody, and promoting the social inclusion of offenders. Social work, with its focus on enhancing public well-being, therefore has a unique contribution to make towards this objective.

Activity 6 asks you to consider further what is involved in this role.

Allow about 40 minutes

Audio CD

### Activity 6   What is it that criminal justice social workers do?

Listen to the interview with Nick Burgess, team manager for Falkirk Criminal Justice Service, who provides a professional insight into the criminal justice social work role, and answer the following questions:

1    How important is knowledge of the law to criminal justice social work?

2    Who is the service user in this area of social work practice?

3    Are there any tensions or contradictions in the role of a criminal justice social worker?

### Comment

You should now have a better idea of what is involved in the assessment and supervision of offenders and an appreciation of the importance of the law in legitimising social work interventions. Nick Burgess is careful to point out, however, that while the law provides the framework for practice, effective work with offenders requires a number of social work skills, including communication, developing therapeutic relationships in supervision, assessment and risk management.

The criminal justice social work task is therefore varied and complex. In part this is because there are a range of 'service users': the courts, suspects, the accused and offenders. Nick Burgess identifies two distinct roles for staff: in the administration of justice and the welfare of the offender. There are obviously tensions in these concerns. On the one hand, criminal justice social workers have powers to control the people who are referred to them by the courts and obligations to enforce court orders. On the other, they need to be able to work with an offender in a way that is holistic and inclusive and which can have a positive impact on their offending behaviour. This may involve providing support and assistance to resolve personal and social problems related to their offending as well as helping them to take responsibility for their actions. The tension between care and control captures one of the key challenges facing criminal justice social workers. Effective and ethical practice requires an ability to consider and manage the needs and rights of all stakeholders in criminal justice, including the court, the public, victims and offenders.

---

The particular contribution of local authority social work practice to reducing reoffending was questioned in 2003 when the Scottish Labour Party made a manifesto pledge to set up a single correctional service agency for Scotland. This proposal, which threatened to undermine the distinctive identity and function of criminal justice social work by allying it with prison-based punishment, was strongly resisted (McNeill, 2005). Nevertheless the Scottish Executive remained committed to achieving greater coordination and monitoring of the effectiveness of community and custodial disposals. They introduced a new legal framework in the Management of Offenders etc. (Scotland) Act 2005, which retains local authority responsibility for the delivery of key services but places them within a new and more centralised organisational structure. Figure 3 shows the new offender management arrangements.

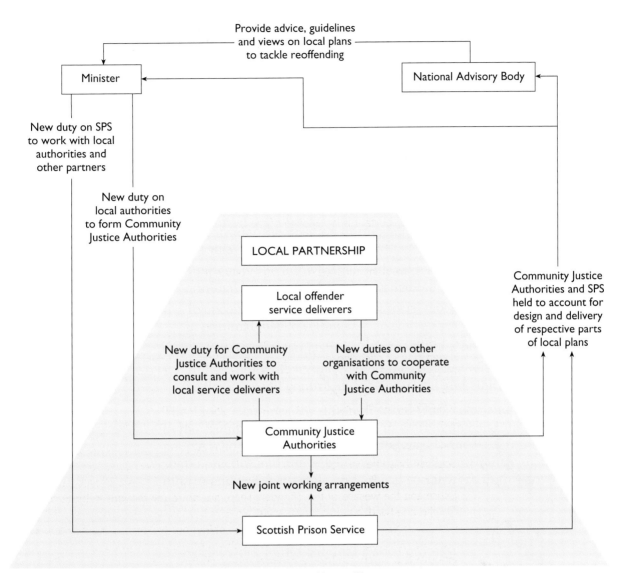

Figure 3    New offender management arrangements (Scottish Executive, 2004b, p. 67)

From 2007–2008 area plans for criminal justice services will be produced by eight statutory community justice authorities (CJAs), which will distribute funds for local community justice services and monitor their effects in reducing reoffending. These plans will be drawn up under the guidance of a new National Advisory Body on Offender Management, in line with the government strategy to reduce reoffending. The CJAs bring together local authorities and other partner organisations (e.g. criminal justice agencies, health boards and voluntary bodies) in an attempt to improve joint working and achieve integrated case management of offenders. Criminal justice social work services have a duty to cooperate with their CJA, may transfer some of their functions to the CJA, and must deliver their services in line with the local plan. Both the CJA and Scottish ministers have powers to direct failing criminal justice social work services to comply.

Commentators have expressed concern that this policy focus on offender management and reducing reoffending could shift priorities away from reducing the use of custody and promoting the social inclusion of offenders, thus undermining a key objective of community-based disposals (McNeill and Whyte, forthcoming). Social workers have a role in articulating the importance of these aims and should not allow the need for improved structural arrangements to obscure their wider commitment to promote social inclusion and well-being.

## Changing objectives

We have seen that social workers in criminal justice settings face a number of demands, including calls for greater punishment, supervision, treatment, welfare, enhancing responsibility, providing public protection and managing offenders.

Changes in the policy context and the legal framework have heightened these demands and challenge practitioners to reconsider and reaffirm the objectives of their profession. In Activity 7 you are asked to read a chapter by Robert MacKay, who reflects on how developments during the past two decades have affected criminal justice social work. This will provide you with an opportunity to consolidate your understanding of the social work role.

Allow about 1 hour

Reader

## Activity 7   Social work and criminal justice

Read Chapter 9, 'Social work practice in the criminal justice system', in the Reader and make notes on the following questions:

*Chapter 12 of Reader + Activity*

1   How does MacKay characterise the policy approach to crime and antisocial behaviour?

2   Summarise what is meant by 'prevention', 'minimal intervention' and 'maximum protection'.

3   How has social work practice within the criminal justice system changed? Does this represent a fundamental shift in the role of social work?

## Comment

MacKay argues that current policy involves many agencies, not just mainstream criminal justice agencies, but health, education, social services, etc., and that it is based on a threefold approach – prevention, minimal intervention and maximum protection.

Crime prevention involves a policy commitment to design out crime. This can be achieved by different methods such as the installation of CCTV or the provision of services to keep young people 'out of trouble'. Minimal intervention refers to the idea that rather than offending behaviour automatically resulting in a court appearance, other less stigmatising and potentially more constructive forms of intervention should be pursued. Diversion and mediation schemes are examples of such intervention. These should be understood not as soft options but as effective community-based responses to offending behaviour that seek to address in a more practical manner the offending behaviour and its causes. The concept of maximum protection recognises the potential tension between public safety and concern for the welfare of the offender. Legislative change has shifted the emphasis towards public protection – MacKay gives the example of the Children (Scotland) Act 1995 and the acknowledgement that public protection can take priority over the welfare of the child (section 16(5) of the Act).

MacKay sees in the many operational changes of the 1990s an important shift. Social work practice within the criminal justice system has moved towards addressing offending behaviour as opposed to meeting welfare needs. There is now an increased emphasis on professionalism and the development of practice impacting on offending behaviour and risk analysis, although the fundamentals of social work remain largely the same. While owing a duty to the court and acting within the statutory framework, the social worker is also concerned to practise in a value-based way in order to promote social welfare and social justice. This now embraces a concern for the victim of crime and the wider community. MacKay notes the rise in influence of restorative justice ideas in this context.

## 1.4 Social work values and criminal justice

Recent trends in criminal justice policy, such as the emphasis on public protection and the concern to introduce tougher measures to reduce reoffending, might seem incompatible with the value base of social work because they focus heavily on a crime control model of criminal justice and have, on occasion, threatened the welfare orientation of the Scottish system. We have seen, however, that addressing an offender's needs and protecting the public are not necessarily conflicting objectives:

> the same activities which help offenders to solve problems of importance to them can also contribute to 'correctional' goals such as crime reduction.
> (Raynor, quoted in Barry, 2000, p. 591)

It has also been noted that the social worker's duty to promote public welfare goes beyond their role in assisting offenders and involves duties towards the wider community, to protect them from possible danger or harm. In this way one of the central aims of criminal justice can be reconciled with the social work role.

This fit is important because in addition to their legal obligations social workers have a professional obligation to uphold social work values. What does this mean, and how can a better understanding of social work values aid decision making within the legal framework? Activity 8 helps you to explore what is meant by values-based practice in this area by considering the role of a criminal justice social worker in court.

Allow about 15 minutes

### Activity 8  Values-based practice

Read the following quote from Moore and Whyte, which comments on the social work responsibilities under NOS.

> Any social worker attending or operating within the court in the exercise of their responsibilities under National Objectives and Standards (NOS) has a two-fold task. Part of the task involves assisting the court and providing a social work service to it, and part of the task involves assisting people in trouble who appear before the court, providing a service to them and their families or others involved with them. There are at times unavoidable tensions, difficulties, and dilemmas in this duality. Nonetheless the two elements in the social worker's task in court are inseparable.
> (Moore and Whyte, 1998, p. 74)

Compare this with the value requirements of the Scottish Social Services Council (SSSC) Code of Practice for Social Service Workers (2002):

Social service workers must:

1  Protect the rights and promote the interests of service users and carers.

2  Strive to establish and maintain the trust and confidence of service users and carers.

3  Promote the independence of service users while protecting them as far as possible from danger or harm.

4  Respect the rights of service users while seeking to ensure that their behaviour does not harm themselves or other people.

5   Uphold public trust and confidence in social services.

6   Be accountable for the quality of their work and take responsibility for maintaining and improving their knowledge and skills.

(SSSC, 2002, pp. 3–4)

Which of these value requirements seem to relate to Moore and Whyte's view?

## Comment

The six statements in the Code of Practice are all relevant but the fourth one gets to the heart of the creative challenge facing social workers. They have responsibilities to people appearing before the court and to the court itself, and these may conflict. Another way of considering this dilemma is by defining who the 'service user' is in this situation. From one point of view the person appearing in court is a service user, but the social worker is constrained by his or her responsibilities towards the court in very particular ways. Thus, the social worker may find that their role as an officer of the court requires different behaviour towards their 'client' from, for example, their role when working in an advice centre or in some other capacity. There are competing rights and demands in this situation, including the rights of members of the community to be protected from criminal behaviour and, depending on the nature of the alleged offence, the rights of other members of the client's family to protection, particularly in cases involving domestic violence and abuse.

---

This activity demonstrates that the tension between care and control, welfare and justice is inherent in the social work role. Social workers have statutory duties and powers to intervene in people's lives and although these interventions will not always be welcome they may be necessary to promote public safety. This is particularly the case in the criminal justice context. Under the SSSC Code of Practice social workers are also required to safeguard the rights and interests of offenders, to establish and maintain their trust and confidence, and promote their independence. These skills are essential for effective practice with offenders but it is not easy to 'combine respect and care with the control inherent in statutory orders' (ADSW, 2003). Such is the complexity of criminal justice social work.

In the final part of Section 1 you are asked to consider how far an understanding of the law can assist values-based practice in the criminal justice process. This is an issue that we will return to throughout this block as you encounter different criminal justice social work tasks. We will explore the relationship between social work and the law through the following course themes, which relate to social work values and have particular relevance in the criminal justice setting:

- Accountability
- Rights
- Partnership
- Respecting diversity and responding to difference
- Empowerment and anti-oppressive practice.

### Accountability

The publication of the NOS and reform of the organisational management of criminal justice social work services was motivated by a concern to improve the accountability of local authorities to central government in the performance of this function. One of the first tasks of the new SWIA in 2005 was to inspect criminal justice social work services and Scotland's Criminal Justice Plan (Scottish Executive, 2004b) made clear reference to the findings of previous inspections to support the need for tighter legislative measures on offender management (see Box 4).

---

**Box 4   Performance inspection of criminal justice social work services**

Reports published by SWIA are valuable sources of information on current social work practice and you will find it helpful to consult the report on your local criminal justice services (a link to SWIA is provided in the Directory on your course website).

The Scottish Executive (2004b, para. 5.9) noted the following weaknesses in the delivery of criminal justice social work:

- a lack of overall strategic direction
- inconsistent adherence to the requirements of national standards
- a failure to implement systematically the main principles of effective practice in reducing reoffending
- variations in the quality of practice both within and across authorities and a lack of systematic performance management.

---

While the intensity of the policy gaze in this area can pose difficulties for practitioners, the legal framework is in keeping with both social work and legal values, as social workers are required to be accountable for the quality of their work and justice demands consistency in the quality of community disposals. Commentators have questioned the appropriateness of setting targets (such as those to reduce reconviction rates by 2 per cent) as a means of achieving accountability and improving quality of performance (McNeill and Whyte, forthcoming). But the objectives themselves are sound.

The question of accountability to the general public is more complex given a level of public ignorance about the criminal justice social work role. This can be seen, for example, in the assumption that supervision means surveillance and popular concern about the leniency of alternatives to punishment. Social workers have an obligation under the SSSC Code of Practice to 'uphold public trust and confidence' in criminal justice services, and the new CJAs are required by executive guidance to develop a communications strategy in their local plans to address this (Scottish Executive, 2006b). It is notable that this strategy includes offenders and their families as part of the audience who need to have confidence in community justice services. CJAs and criminal justice social workers are therefore reminded to engage these end users and to recognise the importance of their views in the development of services.

In considering the relevance of accountability to criminal justice social work practice it should be remembered that criminal justice is itself a form of accountability to the public. Prosecutions are taken on our behalf and are designed to hold offenders to account for breaches of the criminal law. Accountability in itself does not require punishment but does legitimise state (and therefore social work) intervention in offenders' lives. Both the criminal law and social work recognise the autonomy of individuals to make choices about how they lead their lives. It is precisely this capacity to choose that underpins the judgement of criminal responsibility. Those who lack capacity are not culpable in the eyes of the law and this is one of the reasons why children and the mentally disordered may be treated differently. Social work practice in the criminal justice system goes further than this and recognises that criminal behaviour is not simply a choice but may also result from the social circumstances of the offender, factors over which they may have little control. Social workers must therefore assist people to improve their capacity for making choices whilst holding them to account for the consequences of their actions (ADSW, 1996a).

### Rights

We have seen that social workers are obliged to 'protect the rights and interests of service users', a statement that may be a source of some controversy when applied to work with offenders, who are popularly believed to have forfeited their rights. Criminal justice social work along with all criminal justice agencies must now comply with the Human Rights Act 1998, which incorporates into domestic law the fundamental rights set out in the European Convention on Human Rights (ECHR). The two articles of particular relevance to criminal law and social work practice are reproduced in Boxes 5 and 6. However, it should be noted that public authorities are required to respect all of the provisions and if you are unfamiliar with this source of law you should consult the ECHR wall chart for details.

---

**Box 5   ECHR Article 5 – The right to liberty and security**

1  Everyone has the right to liberty and security of person. No one shall be deprived of his liberty save in the following cases and in accordance with a procedure prescribed by law:

(a)  the lawful detention of a person after conviction by a competent court;

(b)  the lawful arrest or detention of a person for non-compliance with the lawful order of a court or in order to secure the fulfilment of any obligation prescribed by law;

(c)  the lawful arrest or detention of a person effected for the purpose of bringing him before the competent legal authority on reasonable suspicion of having committed an offence or when it is reasonably considered necessary to prevent his committing an offence or fleeing after having done so;

(d)  the detention of a minor by lawful order for the purpose of educational supervision or his lawful detention for the purpose of bringing him before the competent legal authority;

(e)  the lawful detention of persons for the prevention of spreading infectious diseases, of persons of unsound mind, alcoholics or drug addicts or vagrants;

(f)  the lawful arrest or detention of a person to prevent his effecting an unauthorized entry into the country or of a person against whom action is being taken with a view to deportation or extradition.

2  Everyone who is arrested shall be informed promptly, in a language which he understands, of the reasons for his arrest and of any charge against him.

3   Everyone arrested or detained in accordance with paragraph 1 (c) of this Article shall be brought promptly before a judge or other officer authorized by law to exercise judicial power and shall be entitled to trial within a reasonable time or to release pending trial. Release may be conditioned by guarantees to appear for trial.

4   Everyone who is deprived of his liberty by arrest or detention shall be entitled to take proceedings by which the lawfulness of his detention shall be decided speedily by a court and his release ordered if the detention is not lawful.

5   Everyone who has been the victim of arrest or detention in contravention of the provisions of this Article shall have an enforceable right to compensation.

### Box 6   ECHR Article 6 – The right to a fair trial

1   In the determination of his civil rights and obligations or of any criminal charge against him, everyone is entitled to a fair and public hearing within a reasonable time by an independent and impartial tribunal established by law. Judgement shall be pronounced publicly but the press and public may be excluded from all or part of the trial in the interests of morals, public order or national security in a democratic society, where the interest of juveniles or the protection of the rights and freedoms of others so require, or to the extent strictly necessary in the opinion of the court in special circumstances where publicity would prejudice the interests of justice.

2   Everyone charged with a criminal offence shall be presumed innocent until proved guilty according to law.

3   Everyone charged with a criminal offence has the following minimum rights:

(a)  to be informed promptly, in a language which he understands and in detail, of the nature and cause of the accusation against him;

(b)  to have adequate time and facilities for the preparation of his defence;

(c)  to defend himself in person or through legal assistance of his own choosing or, if he has not sufficient means to pay for legal assistance, to be given it free when the interests of justice so require;

(d)  to examine or have examined witnesses against him and to obtain the attendance and examination of witnesses on his behalf under the same conditions as witnesses against him;

(e)  to have the free assistance of an interpreter if he cannot understand or speak the language used in court.

These articles protect the 'due process' rights of all individuals before the law and they have been used to challenge inadequacies in the administration of criminal justice in Scotland. For example Article 5 has been cited in cases concerning pre-trial delays, remand and bail conditions, and Article 6 for delays in the trial process and notably the lack of independence of temporary sheriffs (whose office was abolished as a result).

These provisions, however, do not amount to an 'offender's charter', as some critics have alleged. There is nothing in the ECHR that prevents the state from legitimately imposing restrictions on individuals who breach the criminal law or represent a threat to public safety (see the wide exceptions to liberty in Article 5), as long as detention is authorised by law, is in accordance with a legitimate objective and is a proportionate response. A balance has to be struck between the interests of the individual, their victims and the general public. Criminal justice social workers have an important role to play in assessing where this balance lies through an analysis of the risk which offenders present. This obligation towards public safety must be taken seriously and recognises that other 'service users' exist whose rights to liberty and security must also be respected.

The ECHR makes clear that offenders do not lose all of their rights by virtue of their offending behaviour. Social workers also have a role in respecting offenders as individuals and must 'ensure that the offender's ability and right to function as a member of society is not impaired to a greater extent than is necessary in the interests of justice' (ADSW, 1996a). They should therefore be prepared to challenge contrary views in the interests of social inclusion and where possible work towards reconciliation of offenders with their communities.

Finally, in relation to rights, social workers have obligations through the NOS and professional bodies to consider the rights and needs of victims of crime (ADSW, 1996b). Recent policy and legislative initiatives have sought to improve the position of victims whose interests traditionally have been neglected in the criminal justice process. Activity 9 is designed to familiarise you with the *National Standards for Victims of Crime* produced by the Scottish Executive (Scottish Executive, 2005).

Allow about 20 minutes

Website

### Activity 9   National Standards for Victims of Crime

Following the link from this activity on the course website, locate the leaflet on *National Standards for Victims of Crime* and consider how these might relate to social work services.

### Comment

The National Standards do not have force of law but the Scottish Executive has made a commitment as part of their ongoing strategy for victims to monitor and evaluate their implementation. These have particular relevance to victim support services and work within the children's hearings system, but are also important sources of information for use in the support of victims of crime who may be existing service users or carers. Further information designed to support victims of crime through the criminal justice process can be accessed on the Scottish Victims of Crime website (www).

Criminal justice social work services must also recognise and be sensitive to the needs of victims and consider their interests, for example when completing a risk assessment or supervising offenders in the community. Social workers may also be involved with more direct work with victims, for example in victim–offender mediation schemes and other restorative justice projects.

In addition to this policy guidance, victims of crime also have limited statutory rights in the criminal justice process, as summarised in Box 7.

---

**Box 7    Victims rights**

*Criminal Justice (Scotland) Act 2003*

Section 14 – gives victims of certain crimes the right to make a written victim statement to the court, to be considered at the sentencing stage, outlining the impact a crime has had on them. This is currently being piloted in Edinburgh, Ayr and Kilmarnock and may be extended across Scotland.

Section 16 and 17 – introduces a victim notification scheme for victims of violent or sexual crimes whose offenders are sentenced to four years or more in custody. They can register for a right to receive information about a prisoner (on release, death, absconding from custody or revocation of licence) and may make representations to the Parole Board about their release.

---

## Partnership

Criminal justice social work services are delivered in partnership with a range of other statutory and non-statutory agencies such as the police, prison service, health service providers and voluntary bodies (e.g. Apex Scotland and SACRO). Interagency working presents a range of challenges for practitioners who may have different professional values and aims. The Management of Offenders etc. (Scotland) Act 2005 was introduced in order to improve joint working between 'partner' agencies and coordinate the management of offenders, particularly in transition between custodial sentences and community supervision. It imposes a duty on CJAs to establish an information sharing process so that relevant data about offenders is shared between agencies (s. 3(5)(g)) for better offender and risk management.

This can, however, create a value conflict with the need 'to establish and maintain the trust and confidence' of offenders:

> ... tensions can arise between the general principle of confidentiality and the obligation to share information which could contribute to public protection. Criminal Justice Social Work staff require to have clear protocols within which to manage these tensions. The qualities Social Work staff demonstrate in forming and maintaining constructive working relationships can, in turn, act as very effective pro-social models for service users.
>
> (ADSW, 2003, Appendix 1)

Sensitive personal information needs to be handled carefully within the principles of the Data Protection Act 1998 and local agency protocols (see Block 1, Section 2.5). However, adherence to the law alone may not satisfy value commitments. Social workers should ensure that information-sharing decisions are fully explained and understood by the offender even where their consent to disclosure is not required (e.g. where an offender discloses the commission of an offence in breach of the terms of a probation order).

### Respecting diversity and responding to difference

Criminal justice organisations, like other bodies delivering public services, have general duties to eliminate unlawful discrimination and promote equality of opportunity on the grounds of race (Race Relations (Amendment) Act 2000), sex (Equality Act 2006), and disability (Disability Discrimination Act 2005). Individuals coming into contact with the police, prosecution, criminal justice social work or prison services are entitled to the protection of discrimination laws relating to race, sex, disability, religion and sexual orientation (except where they are exercising a judicial function or carrying out court orders). In these situations, however, they may fall within the scope of Article 14 of the ECHR, which for example prevents the right to liberty and security of the person or the right to a fair trial being interfered with on a wide range of discriminatory grounds. The law therefore appears to offer quite extensive anti-discriminatory provisions in the criminal justice context.

Nevertheless, particular groups will be suspicious of the extent to which the criminal justice system is impartial, with some justification. We have seen that the criminal justice process is a human process and is therefore not immune to the influence of prejudicial and discriminatory views. Inquiries into racial discrimination by the police and prison services in England and Wales have raised public awareness of this issue (Macpherson, 1999; Keith, 2006). Research by the Social Work Services and Prisons Inspectorate for Scotland (1998) has also highlighted concerns about the treatment of women within the criminal justice process. The Scottish Executive is conscious of the need to monitor the performance of professionals engaged in the administration of criminal justice and has a duty to publish information to facilitate the avoidance of discrimination on any unlawful grounds (s. 306(1)(b) Criminal Procedure (Scotland) Act 1995). Social workers need to reflect on the assumptions that they may make about different groups in the course of their work and practice in an anti-discriminatory way.

Social service workers, however, have a broader remit to promote equality of opportunity and avoid discrimination than that provided by law. Within the criminal justice setting this has particular resonance because of its tendency to affect already disadvantaged social groups. The targeting of certain types of crime and offenders by the criminal justice process potentially has the effect of criminalising young, poor, unemployed, undereducated men, with experience of the care system, who figure disproportionately in both criminal justice social work and prison statistics (Croall, 2005; McAra and McVie, 2005). There is a complex relationship between social exclusion and offending behaviour that brings into question the 'justice' of our formal responses to crime. The criminal justice system cannot guarantee the delivery of social justice and will often simply replicate existing injustices within society. For this reason issues relating to class, age and their social context are important considerations for social workers and should be recognised alongside vulnerability to discrimination on other grounds.

Does the system discriminate against some groups of people?

## Empowerment and anti-oppressive practice

How might the criminal justice social worker's role be used to address these issues of social exclusion and empower individuals to lead law-abiding lives? In the abstract the suggestion that offenders need empowering, while central to social work values, may appear perverse. We have seen that the idea that social work should address the needs of offenders has been supplanted by a focus on addressing their offending behaviour, but these two aims, which underpin the social work mandate, are not necessarily conflicting. Research into how offenders can be supported to desist from offending suggests that social work can develop the capacity of offenders to make informed choices. It can do this by encouraging their active participation in the supervision/ change process and their engagement with improving their social situation (McCulloch, 2005; McNeill, 2004). By focusing on offender's strengths, rather than their risks and needs, individuals can begin to recognise the value in their own lives, which is an important step towards respecting the value of others. From this perspective assisting offenders to address their own needs is a necessary part of the social work role, and one that is integral to tackling their offending behaviour:

> This would require the worker to act as an advocate providing a conduit to social capital as well as a 'treatment' provider building human capital.
> (McNeill and Whyte, forthcoming, p. 33)

The value of empowerment also underpins a restorative justice approach to crime, which considers the needs of both victims and offenders:

> All human beings require a degree of self-determination and autonomy in their lives. Crime robs victims of this power, since another person has exerted control over them without their consent. Restorative justice seeks to re-empower victims by giving them an active role in determining what their needs are and how these should be met. It also empowers offenders to take personal responsibility for their offending, to do what they can to remedy the harm they have inflicted, and to begin a rehabilitative and re-integrative process.
>
> (New Zealand Ministry of Justice, 2004, p. 25)

Restorative justice initiatives have been growing in influence in Scotland and can shape interventions at different stages in the criminal justice process, as Activity 10 demonstrates.

Allow about 30 minutes

Website

## Activity 10   Understanding restorative justice

Following the link from this activity on the course website, read the factsheet on restorative justice practices in Scotland. How do these relate to social work values?

### Comment

Social work has been at the forefront of developing restorative justice programmes in Scotland, often within the voluntary sector. There are family group conferences in the children's hearings system, for example. Some diversion from prosecution schemes are based on this model and supervision can involve restorative practices. There is a synergy between the principles of restoration and the values of the social work profession. This includes not only the value of empowering individuals, but also respecting their autonomy and recognising the victim's right to choose whether to participate.

We have seen that one objective of criminal justice social work is to assist resettlement and social integration; restorative justice also fits these goals. Restorative justice recognises the importance of addressing the harm done by the offence to victims and the wider community, rather than focusing solely on the offender. Further information on these initiatives can be found on the Restorative Justice in Scotland website (www).

The legal framework actually provides little guidance as to the content of work with offenders. We will see in the next section that the NOS stipulate certain minimum arrangements for supervision and requirements of action to be taken on breach, but they provide wide discretion to practitioners in how to deliver these services. This makes room for creative social work and is where an appreciation of social work values can aid good practice. The law does, however, have an important function in outlining the limits of social work intervention, and knowledge of the law is essential to anti-oppressive practice. As Moore and Whyte remind us:

> The only legitimacy for intervening in the life of the individual within the criminal justice process (in most cases a relatively involuntary relationship) is the individual's offending behaviour. ... If individuals have social needs which require to be met but are not crime-related or crime-producing, or if the offence is not sufficiently serious to fall within the

criteria of the 'twin-track' approach, services should be offered, as far as possible, through voluntary provision ... No-one should be drawn into criminal justice processes in order to receive social work help.

(Moore and Whyte, 1998, p.24)

Rehabilitative intervention is not simply 'help'; it also imposes limitations on the rights of the individual who is subject to social work intervention. Risk assessment and offence-based practice is therefore an ethical approach to social work in this area. It seeks to ensure that 'the most intensive and potentially most intrusive services are focussed on those service users who pose the greatest risk of causing harm to others' (ADSW, 2003). It also seeks to prevent socially disadvantaged people from being drawn further into the 'net' of criminal justice control, which can result in further social exclusion.

## 1.5 Conclusion

This section has introduced you to criminal justice and the social work role in order to provide a background context to your studies in this block. By engaging with policy development and theories about criminal justice and social work, you will be better able to understand the legal provisions and demands placed on social work practice in this area.

In the next section we will explore in more detail the stages of social work involvement in the criminal justice process.

### Key points

- Criminal justice is a contested field of practice that is influenced by cultural, social and political interpretations of 'crime' and 'justice'.
- The criminal justice process is limited in its ability to control crime.
- All social workers need an understanding of the criminal justice process to advise and support service users and their families.
- The mandate for criminal justice social work is found in the Social Work (Scotland) Act 1968, the National Objectives and Standards for Social Work in the Criminal Justice System and the Management of Offenders etc. (Scotland) Act 2005.
- Criminal justice social workers have a dual role: working with offenders towards the reduction of reoffending and informing and advising the criminal justice process.
- There are tensions between the care and control aspects of this role.
- An understanding of the law can help practitioners to manage these tensions.
- Effective and ethical social work practice requires a commitment to social work values and ongoing professional development

# 2 Social work in the criminal justice process

For this section you need:

- audio CD
- course website access for online activities.

## Core questions

- How does the criminal justice process work?
- What is the social worker's role at each stage?
- How can social workers influence the outcome of this process?
- How do judges exercise discretion when sentencing offenders?
- What is a social enquiry report (SER)?
- What approach should a social worker adopt in preparing an SER?
- What factors influence early release and parole?
- What legal issues arise in risk assessment and the practice of supervising offenders?

## 2.1 Introduction

This section outlines the law that is relevant to social work practice in the criminal justice process. It aims to provide an overview for individuals and their families who may come into contact with the criminal justice process, and for practitioners who may be required to offer them advice and support. It also focuses specifically on criminal justice social work, which has statutory responsibility to provide services to certain criminal justice institutions and to deliver community disposals ordered by the courts. We will consider how the key professional skills of assessment and supervision fit within this legal framework and how the demands of the criminal justice context affect the social work task.

## 2.2 Understanding the criminal justice process

> The distinctive nature of Scots law and legal institutions is particularly marked in its criminal law
>
> (Young, 1997, p. 3)

The tendency of the media to portray criminal justice stories from other jurisdictions (usually England and Wales or the USA) has the potential to mislead and to obscure the distinctive nature of the Scottish legal process. As a result service users and their families may lack familiarity with the process, its institutions and their personnel. Scots criminal law and procedure differs from that of England and Wales in many ways. The following list indicates some important features of the criminal justice process in Scotland.

- Suspects and people accused of criminal offences in Scotland retain the right to silence under police questioning and at trial so as not to incriminate themselves. In England and Wales, however, silence can be interpreted as an assumption of guilt.

- The independence of the prosecution (Crown Office and procurators fiscal) from the police is long established. The procurators fiscal are key gatekeepers in the criminal justice system with wide discretionary powers. They are in charge of the conduct of police investigations, decide whether to prosecute cases or divert offenders from the process and which court a charge will be heard in (unlike in England and Wales where that decision is for the court or in certain circumstances the defendant).

- There are three possible verdicts in a criminal case: guilty, not guilty and not proven. The latter is an acquittal and is unique to Scotland. It may be used when the prosecution has not proven its case beyond reasonable doubt but it is possible that the accused may have committed an offence. Its continued use remains controversial because of its effect on the life of the accused and victims of crime.

- In Scotland a jury consists of 15 members of the public and a simple majority verdict (e.g. of 8) will suffice for a conviction.

- Judges have very wide discretion in sentencing an offender compared to England and Wales. All common law crimes (a significant number of the key criminal offences in Scotland that are not created by statute) are potentially punishable with a life sentence. There has also been less legislative intervention in sentencing law.

Figure 4 demonstrates how a person can move through various stages of the criminal justice process in Scotland and the effect that has on their legal status (as a suspect, the accused, or an offender). It also shows the various ways in which this process can be concluded, for example by diversion, acquittal at trial, or conviction and sentence.

Activity 11 provides an opportunity to consider the various stages of the criminal justice process and the decisions that may be taken in an individual case.

*Good for TMA3 - part 3*

Moving through the stages of the criminal justice process

Diverted out of the system

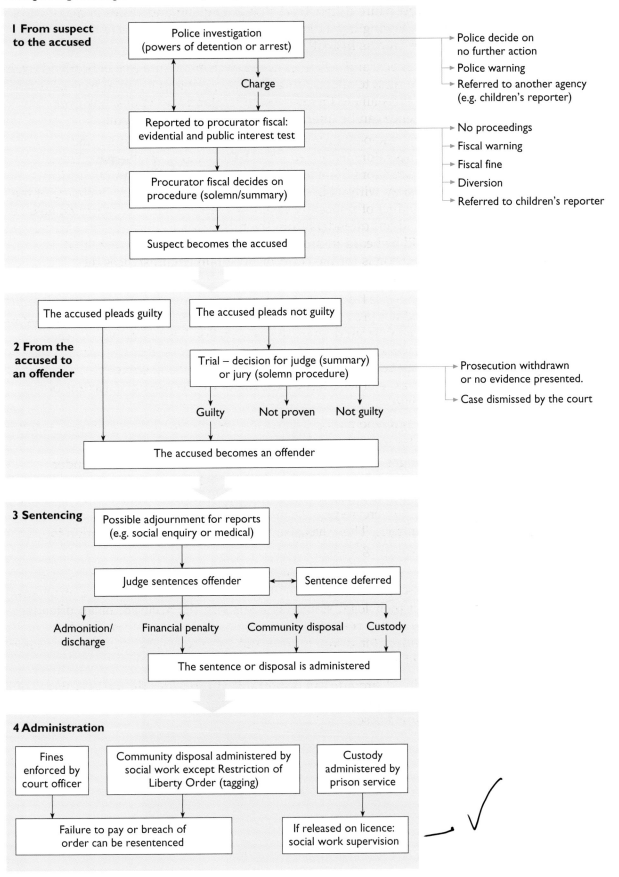

**1 From suspect to the accused**

Police investigation (powers of detention or arrest)

→ Police decide on no further action
→ Police warning
→ Referred to another agency (e.g. children's reporter)

Charge

Reported to procurator fiscal: evidential and public interest test

→ No proceedings
→ Fiscal warning
→ Fiscal fine
→ Diversion
→ Referred to children's reporter

Procurator fiscal decides on procedure (solemn/summary)

Suspect becomes the accused

**2 From the accused to an offender**

The accused pleads guilty

The accused pleads not guilty

Trial – decision for judge (summary) or jury (solemn procedure)

→ Prosecution withdrawn or no evidence presented.
→ Case dismissed by the court

Guilty    Not proven    Not guilty

The accused becomes an offender

**3 Sentencing**

Possible adjournment for reports (e.g. social enquiry or medical)

Judge sentences offender ←→ Sentence deferred

Admonition/ discharge    Financial penalty    Community disposal    Custody

The sentence or disposal is administered

**4 Administration**

Fines enforced by court officer

Community disposal administered by social work except Restriction of Liberty Order (tagging)

Custody administered by prison service

Failure to pay or breach of order can be resentenced

If released on licence: social work supervision

NB Suspects, the accused and offenders before sentence may also be subject to bail proceedings

Figure 4   The criminal justice process from suspect to offender

Allow about 15 minutes   ## Activity 11   Who decides?

Study the flow diagram of the criminal justice process in Figure 4 and, taking into account what you have read in this block, write notes in answer to the following questions.

Who decides to:

1   start the criminal justice process?   *~ Police ~*

2   prosecute a suspect?   *~ PF ~*

3   convict a person accused of an offence?   *~ Judge/Jury*

4   sentence an offender?   *~ Judge ~*

5   hold a person in detention, on remand, or to release them on bail?   *Prison*

### Comment

These are the key decisions that are involved in the criminal justice process from police involvement to the point of sentence (points 1–3 in Figure 4) and you should have been able to isolate the final decision maker at each stage. There are of course a number of other individuals who can influence the outcome of these decisions. For example, you should remember that the police are heavily reliant on the public reporting offences to them, the procurators fiscal are reliant on witness statements and, as we will see, information from criminal justice social workers may be required in order to ensure that decisions are fully informed. The question of whether a suspect, the accused or an offender is entitled to bail is a case in point. Where a bail information scheme exists, social workers may be asked to supply background information to procurators fiscal or the courts in order to assess whether the circumstances of an individual are conducive to them returning to court and not committing further offences while on bail.

The decision whether to hold a person in detention or to allow bail can be made by the police, procurators fiscal and the judge at both trial and the sentencing stages. This reflects the ongoing need to consider the rights of a suspect or the accused in the criminal process (who are innocent until proven otherwise) and the tension with the need to ensure that justice is done and to protect the public.

### Police discretion

Police can detain suspects for questioning

A similar tension exists at the beginning of the criminal justice process where the police have legal powers to question, search, detain and arrest individuals. It is beyond the scope of this course to cover the law on police powers in detail, but social workers need a basic understanding of this in order to advise and support service users, and the general public can be empowered by knowledge of their rights in this context.

Allow about 45 minutes

## Activity 12   Police powers

Website

Following the link from this activity on the course website, look at the Law Resource summary of police powers in Scotland. Then read the case below.

> Leo (aged 19) has been detained for questioning by the police following a fight in the local shopping centre. His mother, Marie, is a single parent with four other children under school age. The family are in receipt of social work support because Marie has an alcohol misuse problem that has on occasion put her children at risk. Marie phones her social worker in a panic having heard about Leo's detention from his friends. They have told her that other people were involved and Leo was picked on by the police because of the colour of his skin (the family is African-Caribbean). Marie wants to go down to the police station straight away but has nobody to look after her children. Although Leo has never been in trouble with the police before Marie is aware that her eldest son has been 'going off the rails' recently and suspects that he has been using drugs. Leo is unemployed and still lives at home where he is a great help with his siblings. Marie says that she would be unable to cope if anything happened to him.

1   Is there any point in Marie going to the police station?

2   How long can Leo be held without arrest or charge?

3   Does Leo have the right to a solicitor?

4   What should the social worker say to Marie?

## Comment

Police investigations can be very distressing for individual suspects and their families. In Marie's case the social worker should be sensitive to her emotional state while recognising that their primary obligation is the best interests of her younger children. Under no circumstances should they be left alone. Knowledge of criminal procedure, however, will assist the social worker in this case. As Leo is over the age of 16 Marie may not be allowed immediate access to her son. Her presence at the police station is therefore unlikely to be of any assistance.

Police powers of detention and arrest are regulated by the Criminal Procedure (Scotland) Act 1995, which places time limits on detention without arrest or charge (a maximum of six hours from point of detention) and on the length of time that the police may detain a person after arrest (with the exception of terrorist offences, they must be presented to court the next day). This Act also provides certain rights to a suspect, including the right to have a solicitor and one other person notified of their detention.

The police can only detain Leo if they have reasonable grounds for suspicion that he has committed an imprisonable offence. Police officers clearly have discretion 'on the street' to interpret what has taken place and factors such as demeanour and previous knowledge can influence whether the police will detain, arrest or charge a suspect. The colour of Leo's skin, however, would not be a reasonable ground and any concerns about this should be raised with his solicitor. The social worker has an obligation to challenge racial discrimination where it occurs, but should not automatically assume that it has in this case.

The social worker should also consider the impact of Leo's possible drug use on the children's care and discuss this with Marie at the next opportunity.

## Prosecutorial discretion

When anyone aged 16 or over is charged by the police, or where after an initial investigation the police think they have sufficient evidence to justify a charge, they must make a report to their local procurator fiscal. We have seen that the Crown Office and procurators fiscal are central to the criminal justice process in Scotland. Activity 13 allows you to explore their role.

Allow about 45 minutes

Website

### Activity 13   Public interest and the decision to prosecute

Follow the link from this activity on the course website to the homepage of the Crown Office and Procurator Fiscal Service (COPFS) (www). This is the office of the Lord Advocate, who has ultimate control of all prosecutions in Scotland, although in practice these powers are delegated in less serious matters to the procurators fiscal. Here you will find information about the role of the procurator fiscal. Identify the factors which they must take into account in deciding whether to prosecute and the possible alternatives to prosecution. Then look at Table 1 and indicate which of the listed factors you think would make a prosecution more or less likely, and consider whether an alternative to prosecution would be appropriate.

Table 1   Factors influencing prosecutorial discretion

| Factor | More likely to prosecute | Less likely to prosecute |
|---|---|---|
| The accused was aged 67 | | |
| The offence involved violence | | |
| The accused was in a position of trust | | |
| The accused is addicted to drugs or alcohol | | |
| The offence was motivated by discrimination against the victim's ethnic origin | | |
| The accused has no prior record of offending | | |

### Comment

In 2005–2006 just under half of the cases reported to COPFS were prosecuted, around 14 per cent resulted in no proceedings being taken and 36 per cent resulted in a non-court disposal. The procurator fiscal has wide discretion over whether to prosecute and must consider not only the law but also the public interest:

> Assuming that the report discloses sufficient admissible, reliable and credible evidence of a crime committed by the accused, the prosecutor must consider what action is in the public interest. Assessment of the public interest often includes consideration of competing interests, including the interests of the victim, the accused and the wider community.
>
> (COPFS, 2005, Section 6)

To do

Box 8 outlines the relevant public interest considerations which are listed in the COPFS Prosecution Code.

*`Procurator fiscal Criteria`.* (handwritten annotation)

---

### Box 8   Public interest considerations

(i)     The nature and gravity of the offence

(ii)    The impact of the offence on the victim and other witnesses

(iii)   The age, background and personal circumstances of the accused

(iv)   The age and personal circumstances of the victim and other witnesses

(v)    The attitude of the victim

(vi)   The motive for the crime

(vii)  The age of the offence

(viii) Mitigating circumstances

(ix)   The effect of prosecution on the accused

(x)    The risk of further offending

(xi)   The availability of a more appropriate civil remedy

(xii)  Powers of the court

(xiii) Public concern.

(COPFS, 2005, Section 6)

---

The outcome of the decision to prosecute will depend on all of the circumstances of each case and you should have found when considering the table that more than one factor is always involved. We will see in Section 2.4 that social workers may be called upon to supply information to assist this decision-making process.

At the time of writing there are three main alternatives to prosecution for adults – a fiscal warning, fiscal fine, or diversion. Reforms are pending following the Criminal Proceedings etc. (Reform) (Scotland) Act 2007, which when the specific provisions are in force will add two extra alternatives – fiscal compensation and a work order. If the accused accepts the offer of an alternative this is not an admission of guilt and does not amount to a conviction.

Although the formal position is that COPFS acts in the public interest, procurators fiscal must always think very carefully about the interests of the victim when deciding where the public interest lies. COPFS has also established a victim information and advice service (VIA) that provides certain categories of victim with advice on criminal justice processes and keeps them informed of the progress of their case. Victims do not, however, have a right to detailed information about the reasons for a decision not to prosecute, as this may be based on confidential information and could expose the accused to further allegations which they would not have the opportunity to defend in court. For example, where an accused is suffering from a serious illness the procurator fiscal may take this into account in deciding that a prosecution is not in the public's interest. There would be a duty to maintain confidentiality in relation to medical records and the accused's health could be adversely affected by continued speculation about their involvement in an offence.

---

## Court procedure

Once a decision to prosecute has been made the procurator fiscal must select the court procedure to be followed. There are two kinds of criminal proceedings in the Scottish criminal courts – summary and solemn. In summary proceedings the sheriff or justices of the peace decide the verdict, whereas in solemn proceedings this is the role of the jury. A solemn court deals with more serious cases and this is reflected in the fact that this court has greater sentencing powers. Before the court proceedings the procurator fiscal will have consulted with the Crown Office and obtained agreement that the offence warrants the range of penalties available under this process. They will also select the court in which a case will be heard. The sheriff court hears the majority of criminal cases in Scotland and is the only criminal court that can adopt either procedure.

Table 2 outlines the powers of the different courts. At the time of writing reform is pending as a result of a major review of summary proceedings by the McInnes Committee (Summary Justice Review Committee, 2004). These reforms in the Criminal Proceedings etc. (Reform) (Scotland) Act 2007 aim to improve the speed and effectiveness of summary justice and will, when introduced, make significant changes to the powers of the lower courts (indicated on the table by italics in brackets).

Table 2   Powers of the different courts

| District court (justice of the peace court) | Sheriff court | High court |
|---|---|---|
| Summary only | Summary and solemn | Solemn only |
| Lay magistrate (JP) | Sheriff (with jury on solemn procedure) | Single judge and jury |
| Minor offences (e.g. shoplifting, breach of the peace, vandalism) | Broad scope of offences, solemn procedure for more serious or persistent offenders, e.g. assault to severe injury, persistent housebreaking | Serious offences, e.g. rape, murder, culpable homicide |
| Maximum sentence – 60 days' custody and/or a £2,500 fine (no community service) *(power for ministers to increase penalties to 6 months and/or £5,000 fine)* | Maximum sentence – summary = three months and/or £5,000 fine (or six months for a second or subsequent offence of personal violence or dishonesty) solemn = five years and/or unlimited fine. *(summary maximum rises to 1 year and/or £10,000)* | Unlimited sentencing powers unless limited by statute |
| Glasgow has stipendiary magistrates who have the same powers as the sheriff summary court | Solemn cases can be remitted to the High Court for sentence if the sheriff considers the offence warrants a longer custodial sentence | The High Court is also the court of criminal appeal. Generally three judges preside over an appeal although this can vary depending on the case |

Around 96 per cent of all criminal prosecutions in Scotland take place under summary procedure. These are initiated by the service of a document known as a complaint on the accused. The complaint contains brief details of the alleged offence. Attached to the complaint is a notice of previous convictions, which are not usually disclosed to the court until after a finding of guilt. Figure 5 illustrates the stages from service of the complaint to sentence under summary procedure.

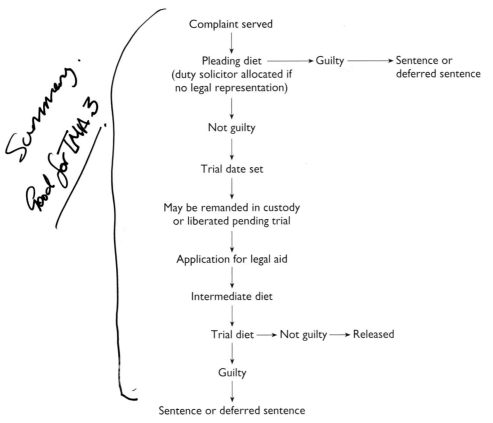

Figure 5    Summary procedure (Fabb and Guthrie, 1997)

In solemn procedure the accused's first appearance will be on petition. The petition will specify the preliminary form of charge. The first hearing will take the form of a judicial examination in the sheriff's chambers during which the procurator fiscal can ask questions and any answers can be read out during the subsequent trial. After the judicial examination the accused will be committed either for further examination or trial. He or she may be remanded in custody or released on bail. Once the accused has been committed for trial an indictment will be served. This contains the final version of the charge and contains a notice of previous convictions, list of witnesses and any productions the Crown intend to present during the trial.

Trials must commence within 140 days of full committal if the accused is remanded in custody. If on bail the trial must commence within a year.

Figure 6 illustrates the steps in solemn procedure from petition to trial. Following trial the same process then applies as detailed in summary procedure.

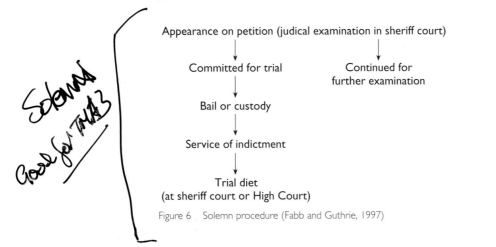

Figure 6    Solemn procedure (Fabb and Guthrie, 1997)

These stages of criminal procedure are quite complex and use unfamiliar legal terms. To aid your understanding Box 9 provides examples of the kinds of cases that will be heard by solemn and summary procedure and which courts will be involved.

---

**Box 9   Solemn and summary procedure case studies**

Case A – 34-year-old man with a history of public order and violent offences. Charged with assault to severe injury. Recently served a three-year sentence for a similar offence.

This case would be heard on indictment in the sheriff court on solemn procedure. The maximum sentence in the sheriff court is five years. However, because of his record and previous history of violence it is possible that the sheriff would remit to the High Court for sentence.

Case B – 40-year-old woman. Minor shoplifting offence, one previous conviction for a similar offence.

This case would be heard in the district court. The maximum sentence would be 60 days' custody.

Case C – 25-year-old man. Five previous convictions for theft from motor vehicles. Charged with two offences of theft from motor vehicles.

This case would be heard in the sheriff court on summary procedure. The maximum sentence is three months. However, the maximum summary sentence can be increased to six months if the case involves a second or subsequent offence of personal violence or dishonesty. Thus, in this case the accused could end up serving a 12-month sentence, receiving two consecutive sentences of six months each.

Case D – 23-year-old woman. First offence, charged with culpable homicide.

This case would be heard in the High Court. There is no restriction to sentence in the High Court. However, if the accused had been convicted of murder rather than culpable homicide she would have been sentenced to life imprisonment, with the judge recommending a minimum length of time that she should serve.

---

Activity 14 allows you to test your knowledge of court proceedings.

---

Allow about 40 minutes    **Activity 14   Leo's story**

Read the continuation of Leo's story (from Activity 12).

---

When asked by the police about his involvement in a fist fight at the shopping centre Leo refused to supply a direct answer and was verbally abusive about his detention. A search of his person revealed that he was carrying a knife. He was arrested, detained in custody overnight and appeared in the local sheriff court the following morning.

*[handwritten margin notes: "Reading diet pleading diet", "SW Nardood", "SW", "SW", "SW", "SW", "Not guilty", "Remanded in Custody.", "legal aid -", "Intermediate diet", "Block 1"]*

Leo was interviewed by the duty solicitor, who discussed the circumstances of the offence with him. He was advised that the procurator fiscal had decided to prosecute him for assault and possession of a knife. At his court appearance, on summary proceedings, Leo pled not guilty.

There had been a number of serious incidents in the area recently in which the carrying of knives was a matter of concern. The duty solicitor requested bail but there was uncertainty about whether Leo could return to live with his mother. Leo's mother, Marie, had reacted angrily when she heard more about the circumstances of the charge and Leo thought that he would not be welcome at home. A criminal justice social worker was asked to check this out for the court and the case was continued pending the outcome of their enquiries. During this continuation Leo was detained in custody and a return date was set. In the intervening weeks Leo found a solicitor (because he did not have a good relationship with the duty solicitor, who had advised him that there was no evidence of racial discrimination by the police) and an application was made to the Legal Aid Board.

At the trial that followed Leo was found guilty of the offences as charged. The sheriff requested a report on his background circumstances (an SER) as he was considering a custodial sentence for Leo. This decision was influenced by the recent prevalence of knife offences in the local area combined with a policy context where the maximum sentences for possession of a knife in a public place have been raised (s. 73 Police Public Order and Criminal Justice (Scotland) Act 2006). Marie was prepared to let him return home and bail was granted. The sheriff continued the case for four weeks to allow the report to be prepared. The social worker was asked to prepare the report for Leo's next court appearance.

1    Using the summary procedure flow chart (Figure 5) to assist you, write down the different stages Leo went through, from the point where he pleaded not guilty to when an SER was requested by the court.

2    Make notes on how social work would be involved at each stage of the process.

3    Identify the social work values that are of particular importance to this case.

## Comment

Leo has been involved in offences that are to be dealt with via summary proceedings. This is because a judgment has been made by the procurator fiscal (on behalf of the Crown Office) that the penalties available under this process are appropriate to the offences committed and that the matter can be dealt with by the sheriff sitting alone. You will remember that the decision about which court should preside over which offence is not linked to whether the accused person is pleading guilty or not guilty. It is based on the procurator fiscal's opinion of the range of penalties available within each court and their appropriateness to the offence. He or she also has to be satisfied that there is sufficient evidence and that a prosecution will serve the public interest.

Refer to Figure 7 to check your responses to Leo's situation.

Offering Leo advice and support during the court process is an important part of the social work role. For example, although he has been able to return home, there may be difficulties in his relationship with his mother and her ability to cope. Where possible the social worker should consider ways in which he or she could facilitate discussion between them, and support both Leo and his family at this difficult time. This is not always easy given the demands on criminal justice social work practice, and support at this stage is more likely to be available to offenders who are already the subject of a court order. The social worker also has obligations towards the court in preparing an SER (which is considered in more detail in Section 2.6). They will have to talk to Leo about his offending behaviour and his mother's suspicion that he has been using illegal drugs. These two roles are not always easy to reconcile in practice, but by treating Leo with respect and explaining their task the social worker should be able to establish a constructive relationship.

**First court appearance**
Leo pleads not guilty

↓

**Trial date set – solicitor requests bail**
Request for bail rejected – Leo detained in custody

↓

**Application made for legal aid**
Leo appoints own solicitor rather than duty solicitor

↓

**Trial**
Evidence heard by sheriff sitting alone

↓

**Found guilty**

↓

**Request for SER**
Leo granted bail on this occasion

↓

**Sentence imposed**

Figure 7    The course of Leo's trial

There are many laws that govern the criminal justice process. Social workers should remember, however, that they are not expected to be legal experts. They should have sufficient understanding of the legal frameworks in order to recognise where an issue arises and know when to seek the opinion of a supervisor or legal professional, or to advise others to do so. Box 10 contains a summary of relevant legal provisions in this area. It is not meant to be comprehensive but will provide a useful future reference point.

> **Box 10 Key criminal justice legislation**
>
> *Criminal offences*
>
> The main criminal offences in Scotland are found at common law and are not defined in statute. The following statutory sources are, however, important:
>
> Children and Young Persons (Scotland) Act 1937 (section 12 deals with offences against children)
>
> Criminal Law (Consolidation) (Scotland) Act 1995
>
> Crime and Disorder Act 1998
>
> The Antisocial Behaviour (Scotland) Act 2004
>
> Protection of Children and Prevention of Sexual Offences (Scotland) Act 2005
>
> *Criminal procedure*
>
> Social Work (Scotland) Act 1968 (sections relating to social enquiry reports, probation and aftercare services)

Prisons (Scotland) Act 1989 (outlines restrictions on prisoners and those visiting prisons, which is important for social workers dealing with prisoners)

Prisoners and Criminal Proceedings (Scotland) Act 1993 (outlines provisions concerning early release, parole and licences)

Criminal Procedure (Scotland) Act 1995 (an important consolidating Act that covers court proceedings as well as bail, custodial and community sentences – its contents have been regularly amended)

Crime and Punishment (Scotland) Act 1997 (deals with mentally disordered offenders, restriction of liberty orders and diversion)

Criminal Justice (Scotland) Act 2003 (risk management and victims' rights)

Mental Health (Care and Treatment) (Scotland) Act 2003 (provisions relating to mentally disordered offenders)

Police, Public Order and Criminal Justice (Scotland) Act 2006 (introduces new organisational structure and police powers)

We will now take a closer look at what is involved in criminal justice social work.

## 2.3 Social work in the criminal justice process

In Section 1.3 of this block you were introduced to the legal mandate for social work in the criminal justice process and have seen that social workers may be involved at various stages, providing a range of services to support the process and those who come into contact with it. Figure 8 illustrates their role with suspects, the accused and convicted offenders.

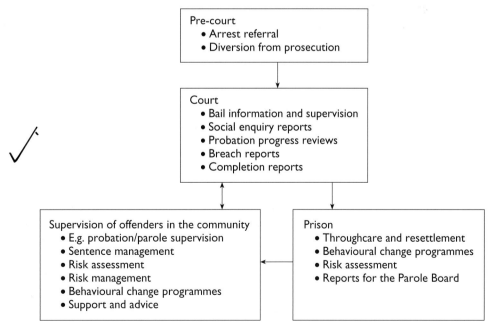

Figure 8   Stages of social work involvement in the criminal justice process

Social work practitioners have their own priorities within the criminal justice process, which are informed both by their legal mandate and professional value base. We have seen that there may be tensions between their priorities and those of other decision makers, such as the police, procurators fiscal and the judiciary. In many circumstances, however, these legal actors have discretion in the exercise of their powers, and through the provision of information social workers may be able to exert some influence on the outcome in individual cases. Fabb and Guthrie argue that in the criminal justice process 'the social worker's most notable offering may be to help to broaden the perspective of all of the players to include social factors' (1997, p. 231). Social workers therefore need to be able to recognise the opportunities that exist for this within the legal framework.

Heery (1996) suggests that in addition to knowledge of the law and social work values practitioners need appropriate skills in order to perform the criminal justice social work task, namely those of:

- interviewing
- interpersonal communication
- information gathering
- assessment and risk analysis
- networking
- advocacy
- report writing.

All of these are skills that social workers use in other settings such as work with children and families and adult care. Nevertheless, it should be remembered that there are particular pressures that arise in the criminal justice context with enhanced judicial and political scrutiny and public interest in the social work role. To help you to make sense of the above discussion Box 11 contains a brief example of what a criminal justice social worker might do in everyday practice.

---

**Box 11 A day in the life of a local authority criminal justice social worker**

09.00   Allocation meeting: SER requests/ orders received from court/ parole licences from prison

09.30   email check/ discussion with community service order worker

09.45   Preparation and planning for SER appointment

10.00   SER appointment with JS, decide you need a second interview

11.00   Phone call from AW, new 17-year-old probationer, to say he slept in but will be down in 20 minutes. Coffee time and decide whether to issue a formal warning to AW.

11.30   Probation appointment with AW – young probationer
Finish at 11.40 or 12.15 – depending on whether you manage to get AW to engage with you

12.30   Lunch (possibly attend lunchtime learning seminar)

13.30   Send out SER appointment letters
Send out formal warnings for non-attendance
Book hire car for visit to HMP Saughton

13.50   Contact sex offender project worker and confirm session plan for next appointment

14.00   Home visit to sex offender with project worker and/or police

15.00   Return to office. Coffee. Write SER report on JS
... attempt to manage interruptions!

17.00   Domestic Violence Groupwork Programme

20.15   Arrive home and attempt to not to over-analyse the day

The variety of tasks and daily challenges facing criminal justice social workers shows that they have to be adept at managing the boundaries in their relationships with the courts, offenders and other service users. They also highlight the importance of social workers having a clear understanding of how the law and social work values shape their priorities.

## 2.4 Criminal justice social work at the pre-court stage

In Section 1.3 it was noted that a key objective of criminal justice social work, outlined in the National Objectives and Standards for Social Service Workers in the Criminal Justice System (NOS), is to reduce the unnecessary use of custody by providing effective community disposals. Not all of these disposals are offered at the sentencing stage. Social work services are also provided earlier in the criminal justice process 'pre-court' in order to support a wider policy of diversion.

Moore and Whyte suggest that diversion within the criminal justice system takes place at two levels:

1   'primary diversion' – measures which seek to avoid bringing individuals before a court; and

2   'secondary diversion' – measures which seek to divert offenders from custody.

They see three reasons why diversion has developed:

> ... economic, social, or humanitarian. A diversionary measure may be established to relieve workloads of procurators fiscal; to avoid 'stigmatising' offenders, improving their chances of re-integration; to help the vulnerable offender, and to treat with humanity those offenders who are not fully responsible for their actions. There is some recognition in these strategies that the criminal justice system is one which can further damage individuals who get into trouble, and often does little to remedy, effectively, the harm that individual offenders have done to others. At a more practical level, the pressures on court business, and the huge expense of court time and of building more prisons as a response to lawbreaking, is once again creating economic motivations to find new ways of dealing with offenders.
>
> (Moore and Whyte, 1998, p. 178)

The police and procurators fiscal are key gatekeepers to pre-court diversion and work with health and social work services in order to divert some suspects from both court and custody. This includes the diversion of children and young people into the children's hearings system and mentally disordered suspects and offenders to the health system (see Sections 3 and 4). Diversion may also be considered to be appropriate for other categories of 'offender':

> where the public interest and the individual interest are best served, not by prosecution and punishment, but by encouraging and assisting the alleged offender to conform to accepted standards of behaviour.
>
> (The Stewart Committee (1983), cited in Moore and Whyte, 1998, p. 179)

## Police diversion

Social workers generally have limited involvement at the police stage unless acting as an appropriate adult (see Sections 3 and 4). One exception to this is the recent development of arrest referral schemes, which are a type of diversion to health and social services outlined in Box 12. These are currently being piloted by the Scottish Executive and are centrally funded through the 100 per cent funding arrangements for criminal justice social work.

---

### Box 12  Arrest referral schemes

Arrest referral pilots are running in Glasgow, Renfrewshire, Tayside, Dumfries and Galloway, Lanarkshire, Edinburgh and Aberdeen, funded until 2008.

They are aimed at reducing drug misuse and related offending behaviour by offering treatment and services to drug-using suspects at the point of arrest. These interventions are entirely voluntary and run alongside the usual criminal justice process. They do not prevent criminal proceedings from being brought but provide an opportunity for individuals to demonstrate their engagement with community services and may provide evidence to support a diversion from prosecution or custody as a suitable disposal.

Evaluation of these schemes (Birch et al., 2006) has found that:

- Pilots were successful in reaching arrestees with substance misuse problems.
- 84 per cent of arrestees would recommend arrest referral to other people.
- Most arrestees were referred on to treatment services.
- There are challenges for civilian workers to overcome in police custody settings, which are not necessarily conducive to support services.

---

## Prosecutorial diversion

Currently, shared working is more widely established between social work services and the procurator fiscal. Social workers can advise the procurator fiscal whether an alleged offender would be likely to respond to diversionary measures by the provision of relevant information. This can be either at an informal oral level, for example information on the availability of services, or can involve the preparation of a formal report (requested under s. 27(1)(ab) of the Social Work (Scotland) Act 1968). Reports into the background of an alleged offender can only be completed with the consent of the individual at this stage. You will examine report writing in more detail later (in Section 2.6).

Diversion from prosecution schemes are funded by the Scottish Executive and targeted on the following key groups:

- those with mental health difficulties or learning disabilities
- accused people who misuse drugs and alcohol

- women (who research has shown may be drawn into custody with relatively light offending records)
- young people (16 and 17 year olds).

*Shoplifting**

The accused is offered the option of a referral to a diversion scheme in place of prosecution. This takes the form of a deferred prosecution whereby if the offender fails to comply he or she can be brought back to court and prosecuted for the original offence. Social workers have a role in supervision of these schemes, which require the person to demonstrate some commitment to changing an aspect of their behaviour that is related to the offence. The schemes can also involve mediation and reparation. The procurator fiscal refers the person to criminal justice social work for assessment and if they are assessed as suitable, practitioners work with them for a specified period, usually of no more than three months. At the end of the period a report is submitted to the procurator fiscal who then takes a decision about whether or not to prosecute.

The cases often considered for diversion from prosecution are minor first offences although more serious crimes can be considered. For example, the organisation Safeguarding Communities – Reducing Offending (SACRO) (www), who run a restorative justice service, have used victim–offender mediation in a case of fire-raising, where the accused had no prior record of offending and had cooperated with the police. Certain offences are excluded from diversion, however, including domestic abuse and sexual offences, where prosecution is in the public interest.

Activity 15 asks you to consider the legal implications of pre-court diversion.

---

Allow about 15 minutes

## Activity 15   Pre-court diversion

Referring back to the information above on categories of diversion at the police and prosecution stages, make notes in answer to the following questions:

1   Is arrest referral a form of primary or secondary diversion?  – Primary  Secondary.

2   Do referrals by the procurator fiscal to diversion schemes involve primary or secondary diversion?  – Both (Prosecutorial)

3   Why are social work interventions at the pre-court stage subject to the agreement of the accused?  — Commit to change behaviour.

4   What implications does this have for social work supervision?  – overstretched – can be frowned by public.

## Comment

Diversions from prosecution are primary diversion schemes and arrest referrals secondary because the former aims to avoid bringing an individual before the court and the latter seeks to explore the suitability of non-custodial options. The distinction between the two is not absolute, however, as arrest referral may make prosecutorial diversion more likely, and those who fail to cooperate with diversion schemes may be subject to prosecution.

The legal status of individuals as suspects, who are innocent until proven otherwise, is important. Procurators fiscal have no power to impose a diversionary disposal; they can only do so with the voluntary agreement of the individual. Social workers have a role in ensuring that people who are referred understand what this involves and have given their informed consent. Acceptance of a referral is not an admission of guilt. Social workers should recognise this and that the choice of participation with a diversion scheme is limited by the possible consequences of refusal and the pressures of being involved with the criminal justice process. In a sense, therefore, participation in supervision is not entirely voluntary. The social worker's report has the potential to initiate a prosecution and this can affect the establishment of a therapeutic relationship.

## 2.5  Criminal justice social work at court

Social workers may be involved at several stages in the court process, providing assistance both to the court and to those appearing before it. We have seen in Activity 8 that this dual role can be challenging. Social work within the formality of the court system can also be demanding on practitioners, who need to understand the pressures of this environment (for themselves, service users and their families) and the roles of the personnel within it.

National standards for SERs and associated court services form part of the NOS. These provide detailed guidance on the social work role in court and outline the role of court-based social workers (reproduced in Box 13).

---

**Box 13 Court-based social workers**

There are a range of tasks associated with providing information and advice to the court and a throughcare service for offenders and their families which court-based social work staff must carry out. These include:

- dealing with requests for reports, making them available to the court, and presenting them in court when necessary;
- providing oral and stand down reports for the court;
- interviewing offenders immediately after the court has asked for a report;
- interviewing offenders/accused persons immediately after the court has passed a custodial sentence or remand;
- interviewing offenders immediately after the court has made a disposal involving social work;
- forwarding relevant information to the receiving prison in the event of a custodial sentence;
- representing the social work authority in the court setting, including where appropriate court user groups, and liaising with other professional groups.
- helping to divert persons suffering from mental disorder who may be at risk to themselves from a custodial remand, either to hospital (in conjunction with local medical and psychiatric services) or to appropriate bail accommodation where available, for assessment (Section 200 of the Criminal Procedure (Scotland) Act 1995). In this context, it is important to establish good liaison procedures with local mental health services and to draw appropriately on the skills of staff qualified as Designated Mental Health Officers.

(Scottish Executive, 2004d, para. 8)

---

There are two main stages of the court process where criminal justice social work input has the potential to influence the outcome of a case. These are when the court is considering bail and sentence. Social workers have no specific legal role during the trial itself but may offer support and assistance to the families of the accused under their general obligation to promote social welfare.

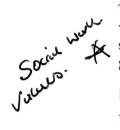

### Bail services

We have already indicated that criminal justice social work may be called upon to provide bail information to the procurators fiscal or the courts, in order to verify circumstances that might otherwise have led to bail being opposed or refused. For example, the suitability of their living arrangements, employment status, and other commitments such as childcare can impact on the likelihood of the accused answering bail. The law on bail proceedings has recently been the subject of reform, prompted by public concern about offences committed while on bail and the need for compliance with the Human Rights Act 1998. Under Article 5 of the European Convention on Human Rights (ECHR), there is a general presumption in favour of bail, although detention on remand is lawful where it is necessary to prevent the commission of an offence or the accused fleeing from the process of justice (art. 5(1)(c)). The ECHR does not, therefore, provide rights to the accused that override public safety concerns. In Scotland release on bail is conditional and may be supervised by social work services if ordered by the court. Bail supervision schemes and supported accommodation are therefore additional functions that criminal justice social workers might provide in their local area. Again, these aim to reduce the unnecessary use of custody by the courts, offering some stability to those with chaotic home circumstances or lifestyles and reducing their risks of reoffending while on bail.

### Sentencing

The sentencing stage in the criminal justice process generates the majority of criminal justice social work. Social work services are central to the operation of the sentencing process in Scotland, through the provision of information to the court (in the form of SERs) and the administration of community disposals (local authority social work is responsible for the supervision of all alternatives to custody, with the exception of restriction of liberty orders or 'tagging'). To appreciate the importance of these tasks, however, it is necessary to understand more about the sentencing decision itself, which is the role of the sentencing judge.

The Scottish judiciary enjoy wide discretion to determine the appropriate sentence in each case. As we have seen (in Table 2) they are limited by the sentencing powers of their court and the type of procedure that is being followed (summary/solemn). Some statutes also stipulate a maximum or fixed penalty for a given crime, for example murder carries a mandatory life sentence, but most common law offences can attract any sentence up to and including life imprisonment. Table 3 summarises the range of sanctions that are available from the least serious disposal (absolute discharge) to the most serious (imprisonment).

Table 3  Sentencing disposals

| Type of disposal | Age limitation** | What it involves | Length |
|---|---|---|---|
| Absolute discharge | – | Imposed if inexpedient to inflict punishment. Not a conviction but may be referred to in subsequent proceedings. | – |
| Deferred sentence | – | Disposal delayed for a period to allow offender to undertake a task (such as being of good behaviour) or participate in a diversion scheme. Severity of sentence affected by success of deferment. | – |
| Admonition | – | Offender 'admonished' or warned. A conviction but no further penalty imposed. | – |
| Caution | – | Financial security is lodged with the court for good behaviour. Forfeited on breach. | Summary limitations apply / solemn unlimited |
| Fine | – | Fines are calculated according to levels (1–5) that are limited by the powers of the lower courts and in some statutory offences. Means of offender taken into account. Fine supervision may be imposed to advise on payment. | – |
| Compensation order | – | For personal injury, loss or damage to victims of crime. Up to the amount of fine that can be levied. Cannot be combined with absolute discharge, probation order, or deferred sentence. | – |
| Disqualification | – | From holding or obtaining a driving licence. Not limited to driving offences and can be imposed in place of imprisonment for fine default. | – |
| Antisocial behaviour order (ASBO)* | 12 yrs+ | Where necessary to protect people from further antisocial behaviour by the offender, a court can impose this civil order with conditions aimed to prohibit acts likely to cause alarm or distress. Instead of or in addition to sentence. Breach is a criminal offence. | – |
| Community reparation order (CRO)* | 12 yrs+ | Where offence involved antisocial behaviour, a summary court can require the offender to work under supervision to make reparation to the community. | 10–100 hours in 12 month period |
| Supervised attendance order (SAO) | 16 yrs+ | An alternative to imprisonment for non-payment of fines. 16–17 year olds must be given an SAO on default. An SAO may also replace a fine for this age group. Requires attendance at a specified place for a period of supervision. | 10–100 hours depending on level of fine |
| Restriction of liberty order (RLO)* | – | Electronic tagging or curfew to restrict movement of offender and reduce their opportunities to reoffend. Free standing order or can be combined with community service, probation or a drug treatment and testing order. Requires consent of offender. | Up to 12 hours a day for maximum of 12 months |
| Drug treatment and testing order (DTTO)* | 16 yrs+ | Where offender has drug misuse issues that require treatment. Free standing order or can be combined with an RLO or a probation order. Requires consent of offender who must submit to drug testing. | 6 months–3 years |

*Could be from a brow user!*

| | | | | |
|---|---|---|---|---|
| Probation order* | – | *(handwritten)* | Supervision by criminal justice social work where offenders are at risk of custody. Additional requirements may be attached, e.g. place of residence. Probation can be combined with a ROL, a DTTO or a community service order. Requires consent of offender. | 6 months–3 years |
| Community service order (CSO)* | 16 yrs+ *(handwritten ✳-)* | | To be used as a direct alternative to imprisonment. Requires offender to undertake unpaid work in the community under supervision. Requires consent of the offender. | 80–240 hours (up to 300 in High Court) |
| Imprisonment | 21 yrs+ | | A sentence of imprisonment rarely requires all of the sentence term to be spent in prison. Most sentences of imprisonment include provisions for early release and some include post-custody management of offenders in the community (see Section 2.7). | Maximum life |

\* summaries of these orders can be found on the Law Resource

\*\* specific provisions relating to children and young people are covered in Section 3

Before you look at the different categories of sentence in more detail, Activity 16 asks you to reflect on the complexity of the sentencing decision and the tension that exists between different sentencing rationales.

Allow about 45 minutes

## Activity 16   Punishment versus welfare

This activity is in three stages.

### Stage 1
Consider the list below and indicate whether you think a custodial sentence is essential, appropriate or inappropriate.

| Offence | Essential | Appropriate | Inappropriate |
|---|---|---|---|
| 1 Stealing a car | | | ✓ |
| 2 Shoplifting | ✓ | | ✓ |
| 3 Rape | | | |
| 4 Possessing a prohibited drug | | ✓ — ✓? | |
| 5 Assault | | ✓ — ✓? | |

### Stage 2
Make a brief note of the reasons for your decisions in Stage 1.

*(handwritten notes:)*

1, ~~Not look too~~ if usual yp - if can be redirected away from Prison.

2, Could be saved by others, diversion - fun, drug habit etc.

3, Protect Public.

4, depends on amount - if intent to supply yes, if small amount ~~no~~

5, Depends on Serious, aggravated etc

### Stage 3

Would your choices and/or reasoning be any different in the following scenarios?

> Sean assaulted a man who was propositioning him. He is 18 years old and has never been in trouble with the police before.
>
> Martin assaulted a neighbour during an argument about car parking. He is 35 years old and has a criminal record. He came out of prison four months ago having served a sentence of twelve months for theft.
>
> Carly assaulted a man she met in a pub when he turned down her sexual advances. She is 25 years old and has not been in trouble with the police before. She is unemployed and married with one young child.

## Comment

The decision to imprison an individual is particularly important from a social work perspective because one of the aims of criminal justice social work is to reduce the unnecessary use of custody. Social workers need to have an understanding of what motivates sentencers in order to write SERs that can make recommendations about the appropriate use of disposals. They should also be able to reflect on their own ideas about sentencing as their personal views might affect the quality of their report writing.

This activity is designed to get you thinking about your attitudes to punishment. For example, you might have decided that any offence involving violence merits a custodial sentence – especially if it entailed sexual violence. Perhaps you feel the same about the possession of a prohibited drug. However, other people might view this offence – particularly possession of a 'soft' drug such as cannabis – as not calling for any punishment at all. This is a subject on which opinion is often divided. When the surrounding circumstances of the offence and the offender are taken into account, the decision becomes even more complex. For example, there may be some agreement that factors such as whether the offender has a criminal record or family responsibilities should be taken into account, but the weight you place on each factor might not be the same. Carly's family responsibilities may persuade you that she should not receive a custodial sentence, while other people might feel that the need for punishment outweighs concern for her child's welfare in this case. Would your answer be the same if Carly was a man and the issue became whether a father should face imprisonment?

This activity demonstrates that information about both the offence and the offender can influence sentencing outcomes and your preferred sentencing option will depend on what you think sentencing is for. There is a key tension between welfare and punishment aims in sentencing and people will come to different conclusions depending on where they feel the emphasis should lie.

Concern about the potential for disparity in sentencing decisions between different judges and courts has led to legislation being introduced in many countries in order to structure this process. Government attempts to ensure consistency in sentencing, however, are inherently controversial because it is a matter of legal principle that judicial decisions are independent of political control. The Scottish courts have largely escaped such interference, with judges themselves responsible for developing a sentencing 'tariff' or going-rate for criminal offences. Sentencing law is, however, undergoing reform following the recommendations of the Sentencing Commission for Scotland (www), an independent body that was set up by the Scottish Executive to, among other things, improve consistency in sentencing. The Sentencing Commission proposed the introduction of an Advisory Panel on Sentencing in Scotland to draft guidelines for the consideration of the Appeal Court on general sentencing principles and the factors to be taken into account for particular categories of crimes and offences. This would strengthen the Appeal Court's ability to issue sentencing guidelines to enhance consistency in practice (Sentencing Commission for Scotland, 2006a).

The Sentencing Commission also recommended that the purposes of sentencing should be enshrined in statute. Box 14 outlines the possible aims of sentencing that were recognised as relevant in their report.

*Good for TMA 3*

### Box 14 Sentencing aims

*Punishment or 'retribution'*
Where the sentence is proportionate to the seriousness of the offence and the offender gets his or her 'just deserts'.

*Protection of the public or 'incapacitation'*
Limiting the ability of an offender to commit future crimes where they are considered to be dangerous and/or likely to reoffend.

*Deterrence*
Where sentence levels are set in order to persuade potential offenders to desist from crime.

*Rehabilitation or reform*
Specialist programmes may be offered to address offending behaviour or to give individuals the opportunity to change.

*Denunciation*
A public statement of wrongdoing in order to re-affirm the boundaries of acceptable conduct.

*Reparation*
The offender is given an opportunity to make amends to the victim or the wider community.

*Crime reduction*
Where sentences are based on research into 'what works' in reducing future offending. This may involve using effective sentences based on the rationales of protecting the public, deterrence or rehabilitation.

*Economy of resources*
A judge may take into account the potential resource implications of each sentencing option including both its availability and potential cost to the public purse. For example a fine may be preferred to probation.

Activity 17 asks you to consider how these rationales relate to the range of sentencing disposals currently available.

---

Allow about 30 minutes

### Activity 17   Understanding sentencing disposals and the social work task

Look back at Table 3, which lists the sentencing disposals currently available in Scotland, and make notes in answer to the following questions:

1    Which sentencing rationale from Box 14 best fits each sentence? (For example, what do you think is the aim of a community service order?)

2    Which disposals are administered by criminal justice social work?

3    Can you identify any connection between social work involvement and sentencing aims?

### Comment

You should have been able to associate at least one rationale with each disposal, for example both fines and imprisonment can be used to punish an offender and may be varied according to the seriousness of an offence. A compensation order is a form of reparation to the victim, and so on. Most of the sentencing disposals, however, 'fit' a number of different aims. For example a community service order can be interpreted as reparation to the community, punishment of the offender (a 'fine on their time'), which incapacitates them during the period of their work, could deter them from future offending and possibly has rehabilitative effects. Research studies have indicated that community service may be effective in reducing reoffending (Lloyd et al., 1995; May, 1999). More research is necessary to determine what it is about community service that meets this aim. Early indications suggest that its benefits might lie in the opportunities for offenders to engage positively with their communities, to build constructive relationships with others and develop the employment and interpersonal skills required to move away from a life of crime (Rex, 2001).

The ability of some disposals to meet more than one aim contributes to their popularity with sentencers, but can also result in conflicting demands being made of them. As we have seen the aims of rehabilitation and punishment are not easy to reconcile and can present tensions for those who are responsible for sentence delivery.

Criminal justice social work is responsible for the administration of fine supervision, community reparation orders, supervised attendance orders, drug treatment and testing orders, probation orders and community service orders. They may also be involved in supervising a sentence deferral and prisoners on release. While there is a strong emphasis on rehabilitation and welfare elements in many of these disposals it is clear that the social work task incorporates other sentencing aims. We have seen that social work supervision involves control and the power to return offenders to court for punishment on breach of an order. Social workers also have obligations to protect the public and to assist the reintegration of offenders within their communities. There is obviously room for tension between these objectives. An understanding of the sentencing framework and the professional values of social work can enable practitioners to negotiate these.

---

The Sentencing Commission report did not suggest 'ranking' the aims of sentencing in order to resolve the conflicts between them. It maintained instead that the purposes to be followed are a matter of judicial discretion and will vary from case to case. The report did recommend, however, that the sentence awarded should be proportionate to the seriousness of the offence. In deciding upon sentence the judge will take into account factors that aggravate (make worse) and mitigate (lessen) the seriousness of the offence and the conduct of an offender. For example, a motive of racial or religious prejudice will always be an aggravating feature of an offence (s. 96 Crime and Disorder Act 1998/s. 74 Criminal Justice (Scotland) Act 2003).

The effect of the crime on victims and the community will also be taken into account. The use of victim impact statements are currently being piloted in Scotland and, while there is no requirement for judges to reflect the victim's perspective in their chosen sentence, they do allow victims to participate in this process and ensure that relevant information is available to the court.

The effect of the sentence on the offender, their family or associates is another important consideration. For example, the defence might make a case that a person in full-time employment would be better serving a non-custodial sentence on the grounds that their loss of employment would impose unnecessary suffering on their children. In making a restriction of liberty order requiring an offender to remain at home under curfew the court must also consider the attitude of any family members to their enforced presence at home (s. 245A(6) Criminal Procedure (Scotland) Act 1995).

Activity 18 allows you to consolidate your understanding of the judge's role at the sentencing stage. You will hear the director of the Judicial Studies Board in Scotland (the body responsible for the education and ongoing training of the judiciary) reflecting on the sentencing decision and what social workers can expect when they are involved in the sentencing process.

---

Allow about 40 minutes

## Activity 18   A sheriff's perspective on sentencing

Audio CD

Listen to the audio with Sheriff Frank Crowe and make notes in answer to the following questions.

1   Why is it important for the judiciary and criminal justice social workers to understand each other's roles?

2   How does Sheriff Crowe describe the decision-making process in sentencing cases?

3   What do the judiciary expect from social workers at this stage?

4   What pressures do sentencers face?

### Comment

Sheriff Crowe sees SERs as a vital part of the sentencing process that enables judges to have confidence in their disposals. He argues that if they are to work together as colleagues it is important for both judges and social workers to have a mutual understanding of their responsibilities and the pressures that attend their professional roles. The judiciary should appreciate the practical time constraints that can impact on social work practice and the concerns inexperienced workers may have about presenting information to court. Social workers should also recognise the needs of the court both in terms of the quality of their reports and where possible the value of a social work presence in court to assist with any enquiries.

Sheriff Crowe observes that there are strengths in the amount of discretion available to the Scottish judiciary, which allows each case to be considered on its own merits. The personal opinions of individual judges may also come into play and it can be useful for social workers coming to court to 'know their judge' so that they can anticipate the problems they may face in their approach and the particular factors that may influence the decision making. SERs should not, however, be written to suit a particular sentencer.

Judges would like to see SERs that clearly set out the background of a person, their attitude towards the offence, an assessment of the various disposals that seem appropriate and contain a clear plan for the offender's future. The reasoning and evidence given in the reports should be consistent and social workers should be prepared to answer questions about this in court. But the judiciary do not expect perfection. Sheriff Crowe describes good report writing as an art, a core skill that takes time to develop.

He also asks social workers to remember that sentencers are publicly accountable for their decisions and that is why they need good quality service to the courts. However, while judges are ultimately accountable for the effectiveness of their practice, they remain independent and are not subject to the same managerialist pressures that affect criminal justice social work (Hutton, 1999).

---

We will now consider SERs in more detail.

## 2.6 Social enquiry reports and risk assessment

### The legal framework

The term 'social enquiry report' has no legal basis but is the common name for reports requested by the courts for use at the sentencing stage. There is a statutory duty on criminal justice social work to provide reports to the court where they are required for the disposal of a case (s. 27(1)(a) Social Work (Scotland) Act 1968). Detailed guidance on the purpose and content of SERs is contained in the NOS, which also outline the legal framework of SERs.

The purpose of SERs is described as follows:

> Reports provide the court with the information and advice they need in deciding on the most appropriate way to deal with offenders. They include information and advice about the feasibility of community-based disposals, particularly those involving local authority supervision. In the case of every offender under 21 and any offender facing custody for the first time, the court must obtain information and advice about whether a community disposal is available and appropriate. In the event of custody, the court requires advice about the possible need for a Supervised Release Order or Extended Sentence Supervision on release.
>
> (Scottish Executive, 2004d, para. 1.5)

The Criminal Procedure (Scotland) Act 1995 sets out the circumstances in which the court can or must obtain an SER. Failure to ask for a report where it is required by law may result in a sentence being quashed on appeal. The cases where an SER is mandatory are:

1   if an offender is already under some form of supervision and commits a further offence, unless the offender is appearing in the district court (s. 27(1)(b) of the 1968 Act); this includes offenders who are subject to:

     probation or community service

     post-release supervision from prison or detention

a supervised attendance order

a supervision requirement made by a children's hearing

diversion to the local authority

2   before making a probation order (s. 228(1) of the 1995 Act) or a community service order (s. 238(2)(c) of the 1995 Act)

3   before making a drug treatment and testing order (s. 234B(3)(b) of the 1995 Act)

4   before making a supervised release order (s. 209(2) of the 1995 Act) or an extended sentence (s. 210A(4) of the 1995 Act)

5   before imposing a first sentence of imprisonment on an offender aged 21 or over, except where the sentence is mandatory, such as a life sentence (s. 204(2) of the 1995 Act)

6   before sentencing a person aged 16 to 20 to a period of detention (s.207 (4) of the 1995 Act)

7   before sentencing a person under the age of 16 appearing in court (s. 42(8) of the 1995 Act)

8   before sentencing a person convicted of certain sexual offences under sections 1 to 3 of the Criminal Law (Consolidation) (Scotland) Act 1995 (s. 4 of this Act).

The courts also have the discretion to request a report to be made orally or in writing where they are not required to obtain one by law.

In High Court cases the court often requests a pre-trial report. A pre-trial report is a type of SER but is prepared prior to conviction and only referred to if the accused is convicted. Prepared prior to a finding of guilt a pre-trial report cannot refer to the offence and merely provides an account of the accused's circumstances. Furthermore, because there has been no finding of guilt social workers are unable to discuss possible sentencing options. Pre-trial reports tend to be used by the High Court to speed up the sentencing process, enabling the judge to move immediately to sentence in cases where an SER is legally required (e.g. people with no prior experience of custody who if convicted are likely to receive a custodial sentence). However, people have the right to refuse to cooperate with a pre-trial report and may wait until conviction when an SER will be requested. Some consider this advantageous because it enables a fuller assessment and consideration of a range of community-based disposals.

It is important to remember that the court is not obliged to follow any opinions or recommendations made in an SER. The court can require the author of an SER to be present at the hearing; for example where a recommendation of a non-custodial sentence is made the court may ask for further clarification. Where they are not available a court-based social worker may be able to speak on behalf of the local authority in relation to reports. Social workers can therefore have a direct influence on the sentence passed. Research suggests that the factors that influence the acceptance of a report's recommendations are the quality of SERs, the existence of a shared understanding between sheriffs and social workers of the criteria for suitable disposals and the inclusion of a 'realistic' recommendation (Brown and Levy, 1998). These factors are rather intangible given the potential for social workers and the judiciary to have different perspectives on the aims of sentencing. Nevertheless, there has been an increase in the number of reports requested by the courts, with a total of 40,265 (including supplementary reports) being submitted by local authorities to the courts in 2004–5, up 28 per cent in the past five years (Scottish Executive, 2006c).

## Preparation of the SER

> Preparing social enquiry reports demands a high standard of professional practice. It requires skilled interviewing, the ability to collect and assess information from different sources, and the art of writing a report which is dependable, constructive, impartial and brief.
> (Social Work Services Inspectorate (SWSI), 1996, Foreword)

Frequently, the preparation of an SER is described simply as 'report writing', contributing to the impression that criminal justice social workers spend most of their time 'writing reports' and not enough time doing 'real social work'. However, it is important to remember that the preparation of a good SER involves one of the core social work tasks – that of assessment. It also provides an opportunity:

> *for offenders* – to consider and begin to understand the reasons for their offending behaviour – perhaps for the first time – and do something about them;
>
> *for social workers* – to consider with the offender whether there are ways in which they can make reparation and whether they are motivated to address their offending and any problems associated with it;
>
> *for the court* – to consider whether a community-based sentence can be imposed which enables the offender to make reparation and which can assist in preventing or reducing further offending.
> (SWSI, 1996, p. 7, para. 2.15)

The time available to compile a report will vary. The law imposes time limits: where the offender is remanded in custody, the court requires the report to be done within three weeks (s. 201(3)(a) of the Criminal Procedure (Scotland) Act 1995), but if the offender is on bail, the report has to be done within four weeks (s. 201(3)(b) of the 1995 Act). In practice there are a number of demands on a social worker's time that can place considerable pressure on the preparation of SERs. Much will depend on how well the social worker knows the offender and their circumstances. The process involves the following tasks:

- reading the court referral, checking departmental records and going over information about the current offence and previous offending
- arranging and conducting at least one interview with the offender and where appropriate members of their family
- checking information through third parties where necessary
- drafting and writing the report
- checking the content of the report with the offender.

When conducting interviews social workers have a responsibility to ensure that offenders understand the purpose of the report, the relevance of social workers questions (e.g. about their health or personal relationships) and the limits to confidentiality of this information. This is important to meet the social work values of empowerment and anti-oppressive practice. The last thematic inspection report into SERs (SWSI, 1996) noted that this does not

Interviewing offenders is part of the social work role

always happen; some offenders complained that the information in SERs was inaccurate and almost a third said that they did not see a copy of the SER before the case was dealt with. The report concluded:

> Offenders should be able to learn the content of their reports before the court hearing and be able to say whether they consider them to be factually accurate. They should know to whom copies will be sent and why. They should be able to retain a copy of their report and be told who will give one to them.
>
> (SWSI, 1996, p. 32, para. 7.6)

The National Standards set out the range of issues that the social worker must address when writing a report (see Box 15).

---

**Box 15 National Standards and SERs**

These are the issues the social worker must address when writing an SER:

- the social and personal history of the offender

- his or her current circumstances, including family composition, housing, etc.

- information about the offence, particularly the offender's attitude to their offending behaviour

- information relevant to the possible sentence, including any information which may assist the court in deciding on a suitable sentence, for example, income, employment, health, responsibilities, etc.

- analysis of the appropriateness of the options available to the court, including some comment on the offender's motivation to change

- assessment of risk of reoffending and what might be done in the community to reduce the risk or prevent future offending

- an opinion on the most appropriate community-based disposal (where possible)

- assessment of the possible effects of the range of sentences available to the court on the offender and on any dependants.

> A report which recommends a probation order should also include an action plan setting out what the offender will be required to do and what services can be made available to work with him or her to reduce the risk of reoffending.

In order to address these issues the social worker must do their research. There is a range of sources for practitioners to draw on when obtaining information for an SER:

the complaint or indictment (i.e. the legal description of the offence being prosecuted);

the list of previous convictions which the procurator fiscal thinks are relevant for the sentencer to know about when sentencing;

the offender's full criminal record (provided by Disclosure Scotland);

outstanding charges or warrants;

departmental records;

the offender;

the offender's family;

other people or organizations who may have relevant information, for example medical practitioners and employers.

(SWSI, 1996, p. 21, para. 5.1)

It is important for social workers preparing SERs to have some understanding of the sentencing objectives that are likely to motivate the court and to frame any sentencing recommendation within that context. However, social workers should be aware of the risks of writing a report to suit a particular sentencer. Social workers must strike a balance between an informed recommendation for a community-based disposal and an awareness of the seriousness of the offence and potential risks to public safety. Thus, although a serious offence, a recommendation for probation and community service may be made for an offence of culpable homicide if there were mitigating circumstances: for example, a woman convicted of killing her husband after years of abuse. However, it would not make sense to suggest a community-based disposal for a person convicted of a violent rape, even if he was a first offender.

The NOS (Scottish Executive, 2004d) make it clear that it is not part of the social work role to prepare any reports that could be construed as an attempt to establish mitigating circumstances on behalf of the offender. This is the role of the defence solicitor or advocate, who may make reference to information contained in an SER during their plea of mitigation. The social worker, however, should be impartial. This means making sure that the seriousness of the offence and its impact are not in any way minimised or explained away (para. 5.5) and that phrases which imply moral judgements or label or stereotype offenders should be avoided (para. 5.1).

Clearly, SERs provide crucial information to the court about offenders' circumstances. When asked about the purpose of SERs, sentencers considered that, as well as informing sentencing decisions by providing factual information, an SER should also include:

*analysis*: for example, analysing a possible association between offending and substance misuse;

*comment*: for example, commenting on the implications of identified health problems for sentencing;

*advice on sentencing*: for example, advising on the appropriateness of the different sentences available, especially those involving social work services.

(SWSI, 1996, p. 9, para. 3.2)

SERs should avoid inconsistencies, contain relevant information, be supported with evidence and any suggested sentencing options should flow from the body of the report. The way information is written and presented may influence the way that a court views the professional opinion it contains. SWIA inspections of criminal justice social work examine reports for errors of grammar, spelling and punctuation that can affect their credibility, as well as assessing them for compliance with the NOS.

Because of the complexity of this task it is essential that social workers approach the writing of their reports in a planned way. Box 16 provides a framework of questions that can assist practitioners in preparing an SER.

---

**Box 16 Preparing an SER**

*Stage 1*

Why have I been asked to prepare this report?

Who is likely to read it?

Does this person already have information about the offender?

What information about the offender do they need?

*Stage 2*

What information do I already have and is it relevant to include it in the report?

What is my assessment of the information I now have?

How can I organise this information to make it accessible to my audience?

*Stage 3*

What further information do I need?

Where can I find such information?

Do I require permission to access any information?

*Stage 4*

Have I provided a clear analysis of the information?

Is my recommendation (if any) viable?

(Adapted from CCETSW, 1996)

---

Activity 19 provides you with an opportunity to reflect on what is involved in preparing an SER.

Allow about 45 minutes   Activity 19   Writing an SER

Read the continuation of Leo's story below and make notes in answer to the questions that follow.

> At the end of his trial Leo was found guilty and the court asked for an SER. You have spoken at length with Leo. He is deeply upset about what has happened and has admitted to you that he was high on drugs when he got involved in the fight. He has also told you that he was only carrying a knife because all of his friends do and he 'didn't want to look soft'. Since being arrested, Leo has not been in contact with his old 'crew' and is adamant that he will stop taking drugs. He also said that he wants to get a job to help his mother out financially. Although his mother is very distressed about what happened, she is being supportive and wants to help Leo in any way she can.

1   Using the framework in Box 16, 'Preparing an SER', and the list in Box 15, 'National Standards and SERs', to assist you, write down the information you would include in the SER.

2   List any additional information you would need to know before you could write the SER.

## Comment

Leo has been found guilty of the offences with which he was charged. Therefore the court has to consider whether a non-custodial or custodial sentence is more appropriate in his case. You will remember that the SER is not a report in mitigation, but rather an important source of information to assist the court in making a decision about sentence.

You would include details of Leo's age, family composition, education, employment history, and so on. In addition, you would provide information about his lifestyle and family circumstances: for example, his substance misuse, his mother's alcohol problem and his contribution to childcare. After speaking to Leo, you might consider that there have been difficulties in his personal life that have influenced his behaviour. If so, you would include this information and an assessment of whether any of these circumstances have changed since his arrest. You would also want to indicate that Leo has expressed remorse for his actions – for example, by mentioning his refusal to associate with any of his friends since the fight, his intention to stay away from drugs and to try to get a job – and to give your view about how genuine this is.

In considering any additional information you require, it is important to know whether Leo has committed any previous offences and to obtain details about these. You must not rely on his mother's assertion that he has never been in trouble before and should consult the information provided by the court and check his record. Normally, you would obtain Leo's consent to contact third parties. You would probably want to discuss the situation with the family's social worker and you may wish to make enquiries with his GP about his drug use. However, you would need to be very clear with Leo what questions you intended to ask and what information you might have to disclose. Often people give consent for a third party to be contacted without fully understanding what information will be shared and how this may impact on them. These issues need to be fully thought through and the emphasis must be on informed consent.

In writing the report on Leo you should be careful not to make any stereotypical assumptions about young black males or an African-Caribbean mother's ability to support her children. Research in England and Wales into the equivalent pre-sentencing reports has suggested that:

> There is little room for complacency as regards the quality of [reports] written on defendants from minority ethnic groups. The review found that of the 484 reports surveyed, only 57 per cent were considered satisfactory or better. Moreover, only 49 per cent of those prepared on African/ African-Caribbean defendants, compared to 60 per cent of those written on white offenders, were regarded as satisfactory. While 93 per cent of the reports were found to be free from discriminatory language and assumptions, 16 per cent of those written on African/African-Caribbean offenders and 11 per cent on Asian defendants were assessed as reinforcing stereotypical attitudes about race and ethnic origin.
>
> (NACRO, 2000, pp. 41–2)

Ideas about race are not the only issues of concern. When making an assessment social workers should take care to avoid discriminatory assumptions about women, people with mental health difficulties and unemployed people where this has no bearing on their offending behaviour.

### Risk assessment

In writing an SER social workers are required to consider the suitability of disposals according to the risk posed by an offender and to target resources in a way most likely to be successful in addressing offending. Since the 1990s there has emerged an increasing preoccupation with the assessment of risk in all areas of social work practice. General guidelines for the management and assessment of risk can be found in *Management and Assessment of Risk in Social Work Services* (SWSI, 2000), although a number of additional risk assessment frameworks have now been developed to aid practitioners in their assessment of particular categories of offender (i.e. serious violent and sexual offenders). In relation to criminal justice social work, the assessment and management of risk has developed from a focus on risk of custody to risk of reoffending and risk of harm (or dangerousness). Angus Skinner, then chief social work inspector, stated in his preface to *Management and Assessment of Risk in Social Work Services*:

> Social work services supervise increasing numbers of offenders who pose a risk to others in the community. Good assessment and management of risk are essential in the supervision of these cases. Social workers are required to assess the risk of offending, the risk of harm that might be caused and the personal and social factors that might increase or reduce the risk of offending.
>
> (SWSI, 2000, Preface)

The document itself states that:

> Risk assessment is an important part of social work practice in the criminal justice system. Social workers assess the risk of reoffending and possible harm to others when preparing Social Enquiry and other reports. They also assess the risk posed by offenders supervised in the community on statutory orders or licences.
>
> (para. 1.1)

Risk assessment is a complex activity and remains at a relatively early stage in its development. However, it is congruent with the shift in focus for social workers away from concern with the offender and his or her needs towards a more explicit concern about public safety and the requirement to view the offender as a potential source of risk to others. Although an emphasis on offending behaviour is not explicit in the legislation, the National Standards state that SERs should provide 'information and advice which will help the court decide the available sentencing options ... by assessing the risk of re-offending, and ... the risk of possible harm to others. This requires an investigation of offending behaviour and of the offender's circumstances, attitudes and motivation to change' (Scottish Executive, 2004d, 1.6).

Thus the concept of 'risk' is now central to criminal justice social work practice. Kemshall (1996) defines risk as 'the probability of a future negative or harmful event'. An assessment of risk therefore involves an assessment of:

- the likelihood of an event occurring
- the circumstances in which it might occur
- who is likely to be at risk
- the nature of the harm to which they might be exposed
- the impact and consequences of the harmful event.

In order to do this social workers use a range of risk assessment practices to help them assess risk of custody, risk of reoffending and risk of harm.

Prior to the introduction of risk assessment tools, social workers tended to rely on clinical methods, or 'professional judgement' based on an assessment of an offender's individual history. Though an important element of risk assessment practice, such methods were open to criticism for being too subjective, providing low rates of predictive accuracy, being open to worker bias and being overly dependent upon information provided by the offender. During the 1990s social workers therefore began to use more objective, empirically-based risk assessment tools (now known as actuarial risk assessment tools) in an effort to back up their statements and provide evidence to support their arguments. Actuarial risk assessment tools consider factors such as the offence seriousness, the court the case is being heard in (i.e. high, sheriff solemn or summary), the offender's previous history of custody and community-based disposals, and whether the offender is on remand or bailed.

In addition to risk of custody, actuarial risk assessment tools are also used to assess risk of reoffending. This type of risk assessment tool is more complex, relying on a combination of 'static' (historical) risk factors with 'dynamic' (criminogenic – or crime producing) risk factors.

Static factors include information such as:

- gender
- age at first conviction
- number of previous offences and custodial experiences
- progress through school
- previous employment
- personal history.

Dynamic factors focus on current areas in a person's life, such as:

- current employment
- personal relationships
- peer associates
- use of time
- substance use
- mental health
- attitude with regard to their behaviour.

These are all areas which research has shown contribute to a person's risk of reoffending (Bonta, 1996). Such assessments enable services to be matched both to the level of risk the offender poses and his or her identified criminogenic needs, helping to target interventions and thus reduce the risk of future criminal behaviour.

The Level of Service Inventory – Revised (LSI-R), devised by Andrews and Bonta (1995), is an example of a widely used risk of reoffending assessment tool that draws on both static and dynamic risk categories. LSI-R is a checklist of 54 factors, grouped into the following ten headings:

- criminal history
- education
- employment
- family circumstances
- accommodation
- associates
- use of time
- substance use
- mental health
- attitude.

Scores are calibrated to indicate levels of risk within local areas. For example, within Edinburgh someone scoring less than 16 would be considered to be at low risk of reoffending, at medium risk if they scored between 16 and 24, high risk if the score was up to 30, and very high risk if they scored 30+. Such a score helps the social worker target the disposal according to the perceived risk of reoffending. Thus, someone with a score of less than 16 would not be considered for probation. Someone who fell into the medium category might be recommended for a standard, no additional conditions probation order whereas someone with a score of over 24 would be considered for probation with additional conditions, such as attendance at a specific group or intensive probation programme.

However, LSI-R and other risk of reoffending assessment tools do not assess risk of harm. Indeed, a person could score '8' yet be at risk of custody because of the seriousness of the offence and the potential risk of harm. This limitation very clearly highlights that effective and comprehensive risk assessment requires the combination of actuarial and clinical risk assessment methods. While actuarial methods are able to identify those offenders who are at a high risk of reoffending, they are nevertheless not good at identifying those who are likely to cause serious harm. Clinical methods are better able to assess the harm that may occur, combining knowledge of the offender's personality, habits and lifestyle with an analysis of the circumstances of the offence behaviour. The risk is assessed on the basis of the offender's predisposition or motivation towards certain behaviours and the triggers that may lead to harmful behaviour. These risk assessment methods tend to be more time consuming, and require the social worker to make a more detailed analysis of the offender and the offence. It may involve, for example, taking advice from experts such as psychologists or psychiatrist's medical reports.

It is important to recognise that risk assessment is not an exact science.

> Whether using actuarial or clinical methods re-offending cannot be predicted, but only a judgement made about probability. There are concerns that offenders may be wrongly identified as high risk, with the potential for longer custodial sentences being awarded as protective sentences; or, as low risk, with the potential for serious offences being missed.
>
> (SWSI, 2000, para. 4)

Research suggests that actuarial tools have an accuracy limit of 40 per cent (Kemshall, 1996). While this can be improved upon through the use of clinical methods it is clear that assessment tools may assist decision making but they are no substitute for professional judgement. Social workers should also be aware that an offender's social disadvantage (for example a poor education or work record) can contribute to a higher assessment of risk. They should be cautious about relying on these factors alone when making recommendations that can affect an offender's liberty.

## Suitability of disposal

Risk assessment therefore does not in itself indicate which sentencing disposal will be suitable for an offender. In order to do this social workers need a good understanding of the options available and must apply these to the individual case. For example, social workers have a key role in assessing the offender's suitability for probation. Despite the terminology employed in the NOS that refers to probation as a 'sentence' of the court, probation in Scotland remains 'instead of sentencing' and retains the rehabilitative idea of providing supervision, help and assistance to the offender as a means of reducing his or her offending behaviour. It has also been noted that probation is now becoming more 'offence focused' in nature and is increasingly directed towards 'tackling' and 'confronting' offending behaviour.

Consideration of the following factors can give an indication of when probation is appropriate:

- the twin-track approach to sentencing (outlined in Section 1.3) which suggests that:
  - all non-violent offenders, except the most serious, should be dealt with in the community (probation then would be one of the community disposals for consideration)
  - all violent offenders, except the less serious, are likely to face custody as a means of protecting the public (this would suggest that probation should be a consideration for less serious violent offenders)

- that the offending behaviour can be linked to specific problems or needs (now termed 'criminogenic' needs) that would provide a focus for probation intervention
- that the pattern of offending behaviour is serious and frequent enough to merit probation intervention – for example, a first time offender charged with breach of the peace may have a number of personal or social problems, but if these are not directly linked to the offence behaviour, or the risk of future offending, then probation intervention may risk 'up-tariffing' the individual when other community disposals are more appropriate (i.e. a fine or a deferred sentence)
- that the offender demonstrates a basic level of motivation to change his or her offending behaviour and to address their related problems or needs.

Writers of SERs should also remember that they need to bring local schemes that may not be operating in other probation areas to the attention of the sentencing judge. As Sheriff Crowe noted in his audio interview, travelling sheriffs may not be familiar with new initiatives provided by criminal justice social work and their partner agencies in different areas of the country. (Up-to-date information on all court disposals, including local initiatives, can be found on the Sentencing Information for Scotland website, listed in the course Directory.)

Box 17 provides some illustrations of when probation and other community disposals might be considered.

---

**Box 17  Community disposal case studies**

Case A – 23-year-old repeat shoplifter with no history of violent behaviour who is shoplifting to fund her moderate drug misuse.

Probation would be considered, with the emphasis on changing the pattern of offending behaviour and providing assistance to address her drug misuse. This would be a community-based disposal, rather than an alternative to custody according to the twin-track model. A drug treatment and testing order could also be considered where testing is necessary to supervise compliance.

Case B – 32 year old convicted of serious assault, no previous convictions.

Although this is a serious offence, it appears to be an isolated incident and therefore community service would be considered as an alternative to custody.

Case C – 25 year old convicted of three cases of assault and robbery, history of violent behaviour.

It is likely that this person is facing a custodial sentence. He has been convicted of a violent offence and has a history of similar behaviour. He poses a risk to public safety. This should be acknowledged in the SER. Possible alternatives to custody would include probation, with a condition of unpaid work and possible attendance at a specialist programme. A restriction of liberty order would also be considered.

Case D – 47 year old convicted of assault to his partner, three similar previous convictions.

Again it is likely that this person is facing a custodial sentence. Whereas Case C posed a risk to public safety Case D poses a specific risk to his partner. Probation with attendance at a domestic abuse programme would therefore be considered. This would be used as an alternative to custody. However, a similar recommendation could be made for someone with no history of domestic violence but convicted of a minor assault on their partner (e.g. pushing and verbally abusing). In such a case probation would be offered as a community-based disposal as it is likely that although the person is not at risk of custody, his behaviour needs to be challenged to prevent him from committing similar offences in the future.

It is important that social workers discuss possible sentencing outcomes with the offender in order to prepare them appropriately – particularly where they may be required to consent to a community-based order and are at risk of custody.

## 2.7 Custodial sentences and throughcare

The offenders most likely to receive a custodial sentence are those convicted of violent offences, especially if there is no viable community-based alternative. Activity 20 looks at when a custodial sentence may be necessary.

Allow about 40 minutes    **Activity 20    David's story**

Reread Table 2, which outlines the sentencing powers of the different criminal courts in Scotland. Then read the case below and make notes in answer to the questions that follow it.

David (aged 30) was involved in a fight in a local pub. It would appear that this was an unprovoked attack on a bartender, who had a glass broken in his face. The man suffered severe facial injuries that required stitches and spent several days in hospital. The medical prognosis was that he was likely to suffer permanent scarring and might require further treatment. The bartender was so traumatised by the attack that he was unable to return to work.

David had a history of offending, including housebreaking and assault. Most of his offences were committed while he was under the influence of alcohol. He was unemployed, having never had a consistent work pattern. He had been married but had separated from his wife and two children some four years earlier, following repeated incidents of alcohol abuse and domestic violence. He moved around a lot after the break-up of his marriage and eventually moved into a council-run hostel for homeless men. The staff at the hostel became increasingly concerned by David's erratic behaviour. It seemed unlikely that he could remain there much longer.

Following his arrest, David was charged with serious assault and detained in custody overnight. He appeared in the sheriff court 'on petition' and pleaded not guilty to the charge. He was remanded in custody for eight days for further enquiries. At the full committal hearing, he was refused bail on the grounds that his permanent address seemed to be in jeopardy and he had a fairly serious criminal record. The court therefore decided to detain him in custody pending his trial. After some 12 weeks in prison on remand, David appeared before a sheriff and jury and was found guilty of serious assault. The sheriff indicated that he was considering a custodial sentence and, as David had not been imprisoned before, the sheriff called for an SER.

1    Why might the sheriff be contemplating imposing a custodial sentence on David?

2    What is the maximum sentence the sheriff court can impose?

3    What more can the sheriff court do if it feels this is insufficient?

## Comment

The fact that David was found guilty of an offence of violence might well prompt the sheriff to impose a custodial sentence. This is a serious offence and his previous record of offending would be considered an aggravating factor. He was aged over 21 and there is little in his social circumstances that might have persuaded the sheriff to consider a community sentence.

The sheriff court can impose a maximum sentence of five years' imprisonment. When imposing a sentence of imprisonment the court must take into account the period of time that David has spent on remand awaiting trial and sentence.

If the sheriff court considers that is insufficient punishment, it can remit the case to the High Court, which has greater sentencing powers.

In recent years there has been considerable debate over whether prison works. While custody may be necessary in some cases in order to protect the public or adequately punish an offender, it is also recognised that custodial sentences should be used 'sparingly'. This is because they are a costly disposal, on both the public purse and the lives of offenders and their families. Research shows that imprisonment fractures the social ties that are necessary to prevent reoffending and can impact on prisoners' families by, for example, damaging the future prospects of their children. Despite an apparent consensus on the negative effects of imprisonment and major investment in community sentences, Scotland continues to have very high rates of imprisonment compared with other countries in Europe. The use of custody has been increasing over the past decade as Figure 9 (overleaf) illustrates.

It is clear that although fines are the most favoured sentence, their use declined between 1995 and 2005. During the same period the use of the higher tariff custodial and community disposals have increased, but the growth in community sanctions has not significantly displaced the use of custody. When these statistics are broken down further a more worrying picture emerges. Over 80 per cent of all custodial sentences

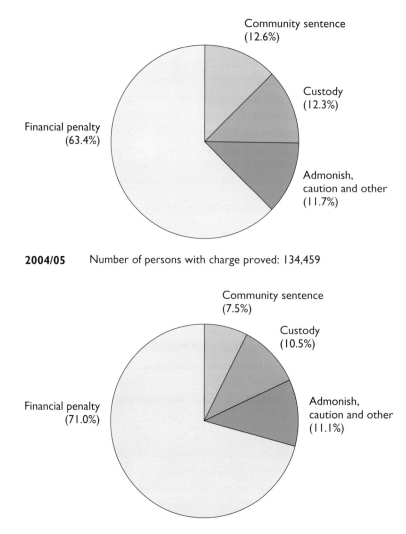

**2004/05**      Number of persons with charge proved: 134,459

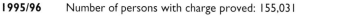

**1995/96**      Number of persons with charge proved: 155,031

Figure 9     Penalties imposed in Scottish Courts in 2004/5 and 1995/6 (Scottish Executive, 2006a, p. 1)

imposed by the courts in 2005/6 were for six months or less. These short-term sentences have become widely discredited for their failure to impact on reoffending, as First Minister Jack McConnell acknowledged in a speech to Apex Scotland (www) in 2003:

> Despite major investment of money, resources and time in community sentences, the prison population is rising and most of the sentences are for less than 6 months. Sentences where we know with absolute certainty that the prisons can do nothing more than 'process' the individual. No programmes for changed behaviour, no time to tackle the drug or debt problems or the violence that characterised the crime in the first place – and will do so, again and again.

(McConnell, 2003)

These trends persist even though before an offender can be sentenced to a period of custody for the first time (unless the sentence is mandatory imprisonment, e.g. in murder cases), the sentencer must consider the circumstances of the offender and in addition must be of the opinion that no other kind of sentence is appropriate (Criminal Procedure (Scotland) Act 1995 s. 204(2)). While this decision (and the power to reduce the unnecessary use of custody) ultimately lies with the sentencer, social workers have a critical role to play in influencing the judiciary and in targeting credible community-based disposals to those repeat offenders most likely to receive short custodial sentences.

The number of women in Scotland who are given short custodial sentences is also a matter of some concern. While most prisoners are male, there has been a rapid increase in the female prison population (up 62 per cent between 1993 and 2002). There is evidence to suggest that many of the women who are sent to prison have committed less serious offences and pose a lower risk to the public than their male counterparts. A large number of women are received into custody on remand each year who do not go on to receive a custodial sentence, and more women have been sent to prison for fine default than as part of a direct sentence (Scottish Executive, 2002a). There are a variety of reasons for this, including social disadvantage, the limited provision of appropriate community disposals for women, and the possibility of discrimination against petty persistent female offenders (who may be perceived as doubly deviant for breaking the law and offending against the stereotype of women's law abiding nature). Whatever the cause, it is important that social workers recognise that women can suffer disproportionately from the use of imprisonment, and support diversionary programmes where appropriate.

Social workers also have a key role to play post-sentence. In addition to assisting those who are admitted to custody to deal with the experience of imprisonment, social workers are involved in preparing offenders for reintegration on release from custody and supporting them through this process. Recent policy directives have made this often overlooked social work contribution more explicit in recent years, placing responsibility on all agencies involved (i.e. prisons, criminal justice social work and other voluntary agencies who work directly with offenders) to adopt a better integrated, collaborative and coherent approach to the goal of reduced reoffending via the effective reintegration of offenders into their communities. We will return to this throughcare role after first considering the legal framework for custodial sentences.

## What does a sentence of imprisonment mean?

Offenders sentenced to a term of imprisonment rarely spend the whole of their sentence in prison; most will be released before the end of their term and this period in the community forms part of their sentence. There are three main categories of custodial sentence in Scotland:

- short fixed-term sentences of under four years
- long fixed-term sentences of four years or over, and
- life sentences.

At the time of writing the law in this area is undergoing major reform aimed to increase the effectiveness of short-term sentences by making release subject to a risk assessment and imposing supervision on the community part of the sentence. The proposed changes follow a report of the Sentencing Commission into the release and post-custody management of offenders (Sentencing Commission for Scotland, 2006b) and are part of the Scottish Executive's overall strategy to reduce reoffending. If passed, the Custodial Sentences and Weapons (Scotland) Bill 2006 will have a significant impact on the workload of criminal justice social workers, who will have an increased role in the assessment of all prisoners for release and face a growth in demand for post-custody supervision. Information on the status of this legislation will be included in future course updates.

The current law on releasing offenders from custody is set out in the Prisoners and Criminal Proceedings (Scotland) Act 1993 and outlined below. (This will remain of relevance for practitioners even if the law is changed because new legislation on sentences cannot have retroactive effect. This means prisoners sentenced before the law is introduced will be subject to the existing arrangements.)

*Short-term custodial sentences*

Custodial sentences that are short-term, that is under four years, allow for the automatic early release of prisoners into the community half way through a prisoner's sentence. For example, if someone has been sentenced to eighteen months, he or she must be released once nine months of the sentence has been served. In most cases the release of short-term prisoners will also be unconditional. However, the offender remains 'at risk of custody'; if another offence is committed that is punishable by imprisonment, the individual can be returned to serve the unexpired period of the sentence under section 16 of the Prisoners and Criminal Proceedings (Scotland) Act 1993.

Sex offenders who are sentenced for between six months and four years are not given unconditional release. After returning to the community at the half-way stage they are subject to supervision under licence until the end of their sentence (section 1AA of the Prisoners and Criminal Proceedings (Scotland) Act).

This 'automatic' early release is controversial because it does not allow for a risk assessment to be made at the point of release and where there are no conditions on the release it also means that offenders do not get the benefit of post-release supervision.

However, if the court feels that the offender poses a risk to the public at the sentencing stage, it has the option of making them subject to the following orders on their release from custody:

*Supervised release order*

The court may impose a supervised release order (SRO) (s. 209 of the Criminal Procedure (Scotland) Act 1995) on some offenders. There are conditions that must be met. The case must be heard on indictment, the sentence must be of less than four years for a non-sexual offence and it must be considered that the offender may be a risk to the public on release. An SRO is only made after an SER has been written and the risk factor is something which the social worker will have had to address in the report. When the SRO comes into force, the individual comes under the supervision of the local authority social work service. The order cannot run for more than 12 months after the date of release or half of the sentence duration, whichever is shorter. It therefore cannot run beyond the date when the sentence would expire, and it is subject to conditions and breach proceedings.

*Extended sentence*

Under section 210A of the Criminal Procedure (Scotland) Act 1995 the court has the power to impose an extended sentence, that is an additional period of post-release supervision that can be imposed on violent and sexual offenders where the court considers it necessary in order to protect the public from serious harm. An extended sentence can only be imposed on violent offenders who are sentenced to four years or more. However, it can be imposed on short and long-term prisoners who have been convicted of sexual offences.

The extension period for both violent and sexual offences cannot be for more than ten years. This extended sentence will be treated in the same way as a licence under the Prisoners and Criminal Proceedings (Scotland) Act 1993, so the Parole Board may set conditions for release for long-term prisoners (see below). Because of the risk posed by such prisoners, the potential length of post-release supervision and the possibility of recall to custody, particular emphasis is placed on the continuity of social work involvement throughout the period of sentence and on the need for close liaison and information sharing between social work services and the Scottish Prison Service at all stages.

### Long-term custodial sentences

Custodial sentences imposed for four years or more are designated as long-term sentences. There are different rules regulating those serving long-term but not life sentences.

The long-term prisoner is one serving four years or more in aggregate. They qualify for parole licence consideration after half sentence and then annually until they have less than sixteen months left to serve. Application is made to the Parole Board for Scotland (www), an independent body that decides whether imprisonment is necessary in order to protect the public and, if a person is suitable for release, their licence conditions.

The Parole Board will take into account such matters as:

- the nature and circumstances of the offence
- the person's conduct since sentence
- the likelihood of the person committing another offence if on licence
- what the person intends to do on release
- any information made available to the board by the Scottish ministers.

Prisoners who have been refused parole at an earlier stage will be eligible for early release two-thirds of the way through their sentence. Those released at this stage will be on a non-parole licence. This means that the remainder of the sentence will be served in the community under the supervision of a social worker.

If a long- or short-term prisoner commits another offence punishable by imprisonment during the release period, he or she can be returned to prison to serve all or part of the unexpired portion of the original sentence (section 16 of the 1993 Act).

### Life sentences

There are three types of 'life' sentence in Scotland. The oldest are the mandatory life sentence (for murder) and the discretionary life sentence (that can be given for a range of serious common law offences, e.g. armed robbery). Since 2006 a new life sentence has been available – the order for lifelong restriction (OLR) (s. 210F Criminal Procedure (Scotland) Act 1995). This was introduced by the Criminal Justice (Scotland) Act 2003 in order to tighten up the supervision requirements for offenders who have been assessed as posing a high risk to the public. The conditions for the use of an OLR are outlined in Box 18.

**Box 18 Order for lifelong restriction**

Where the High Court is to sentence an offender who has been convicted of

- a sexual offence
- a violent offence
- an offence that endangers life (other than murder), or
- an offence which indicates the propensity of the offender to commit one of the above,

it is required to make a risk assessment order.

This provides for a person who is accredited by the Risk Management Authority to compile a risk assessment report in order to appraise the risk that the offender poses in the community. The Risk Management Authority (www) is a new body empowered to research, issue guidelines and promote effective management of risk in Scotland. Social workers can apply to become accredited risk managers but this role is not limited to a particular profession and can include, for example, persons qualified in psychology or psychiatry.

Where the risk assessment indicates a likelihood that the person could 'seriously endanger the lives, or physical or psychological well-being, of members of the public at large' the court may make an OLR. This is an indeterminate sentence of imprisonment where, like the other life sentences, the judge must set a minimum period that the offender will spend in custody for the purposes of deterrence and punishment, before they can be considered for release.

All life prisoners are released on life licence. Mandatory life prisoners may be referred to the Parole Board after consultation with the Lord Justice General (Scotland's senior judge) and the trial judge if he or she is available. Discretionary life prisoners and prisoners subject to an OLR may be considered for parole only after they have served the period stipulated by the trial judge. If the Parole Board decides not to direct the release of a prisoner, it must give reasons in writing and a date must be fixed for the case to be referred back to the board.

A life licence lasts, as the name implies, for life. There are standard conditions attached to such licences:

- The individual must be under the supervision of a relevant officer of the local authority.
- He or she must comply with any requirements the officer may specify for the purposes of supervision.

Other conditions can be added. Offenders who are on an OLR will already have been issued with a risk management plan that requires the collaboration of criminal justice social work, the prison service and health service providers to coordinate the arrangements for the management of the risks they pose both in custody and after release. If the licensee commits another offence, which is punishable by imprisonment, he or she can be returned to prison.

Because of the addition of various orders to protect the public, the law on custodial sentences has become rather complex. Table 4 provides a summary of these provisions.

**Table 4   Summary of custodial sentences**

**Short-term**

| *Under 12 months* | *Over 12 months and under 4 years* |
|---|---|
| No order and release at half-way point of sentence. Sex offenders could be subject to an extended sentence and where the sentence is six months to four years will be released on licence. | Release at half-way point. Possibility of court order, i.e. a supervised release order or in the case of sex offenders an extended sentence. |

**Long-term**

| *Over 4 years but not life* | *Life sentences* |
|---|---|
| Consideration for parole at half-way point. If unsuccessful released on non-parole licence at two-thirds point. Violent or sexual offenders may also be subject to an extended sentence. | Mandatory life prisoners considered for parole following consultation with Lord Justice General. Discretionary life and order for lifelong restriction prisoners considered for parole after they have served period stipulated by trial judge at point of sentence. |

In addition, low risk prisoners nearing the end of their sentence may be released before the half-way point under an electronically monitored home detention curfew (HDC). This is a form of executive release designed to relieve pressure on the prison population and provide an incentive for good behaviour. Both short-term and long-term prisoners may be released under HDC, although long-term prisoners must first have received the approval of the Parole Board.

Activity 21 provides you with an opportunity to consolidate your understanding of custodial sentences.

---

Allow about 20 minutes

## Activity 21   Custodial sentencing and early release of prisoners

With reference to the sections on custodial sentencing and early release above, make notes in answer to the following questions:

1    Which prisoners are classed as short term and which are long term?

2    At what stage are long-term prisoners eligible for parole?

### Comment

All short-term prisoners are entitled to release when they have served half of their sentence. The majority are released unconditionally with the exception of sex offenders sentenced to between six months and four years, offenders subject to a supervised release order or an extended sentence and children who are released on licence (see Section 3.7). Short-term prisoners may ask for advice, guidance and assistance from the social work department up to twelve months after their release.

Long-term prisoners, having served half of their sentence, are entitled to be considered for parole. If an offender was convicted of a sexual or violent offence, the court may have made an extended sentence. The effect of this for a long-term prisoner is that the parole licence period will be followed by the extended sentence period of additional supervision. Parole means that the prisoner completes his or her sentence in the community, but if there is a breach of the conditions of parole (e.g. committing another offence, or failing to keep in touch with the supervising officer) the parolee can be recalled to prison. A prisoner has to apply for parole and as part of the process a dossier of information will be prepared to assist the Parole Board in its decision making. This dossier will include reports from the prison staff and from other professionals who know the prisoner.

We will now consider the social work role at this stage in more detail.

### Throughcare

The term 'throughcare' is defined in the NOS Standards for Throughcare as follows:

> The term 'throughcare' is used to denote the provision of a range of social work and associated services to prisoners and their families from the point of sentence or remand, during the period of imprisonment and following release into the community. These services are primarily concerned to assist prisoners to prepare for release, and to help them to resettle in the community, within the law, whether required by statute as part of a licence or because the prisoner seeks such a service.
>
> (Scottish Executive 2004e, para. 1)

Throughcare services include services to offenders while they are in prison as well as when they are released back into the community, and are offered both on a voluntary basis and as part of a legal requirement.

Section 27(1)(b) of the Social Work (Scotland) Act 1968 places a duty on every local authority to provide supervision, advice, guidance and assistance for people in their area who, following their release from prison or detention, are required to be under supervision (e.g. parole or a supervised release order). Section 27(1)(c) of this Act also says that it is a function of the local authority to provide advice, guidance and assistance to people in its area who, within twelve months of their release from prison or detention, request such help.

While throughcare has long been a core element of the criminal justice social work task, recent policy developments – in particular recent concerns to develop more 'effective and integrated services for managing offenders' (Scottish Executive, 2004a) – have placed greater emphasis on the strategic role of throughcare in supporting offenders to successfully reintegrate into their communities as law-abiding citizens. In achieving these aims, the Executive has introduced a new throughcare strategy to improve the system of community support for prisoners when they are released and legislative changes to require the Scottish Prison Service (www) and local authorities to work more closely together to manage offenders seamlessly and reduce reoffending. A system of integrated case management (ICM) is now in place for all offenders in order to meet statutory requirements (s. 10-11 Management of Offenders etc. (Scotland) Act in relation to certain violent and sexual offenders). In this respect the principal aim of throughcare services remains public protection and, more specifically, breaking the now well-documented cycle of repeat offending.

Throughcare services start at the point of remand to custody or the post-sentence interview by a court-based social worker. National standards stress the importance of contact being established between criminal justice social work, prisoners and their families as soon as possible, in order for throughcare to be effective. On reception into prison this contact passes to the prison-based social worker. It is important that information obtained in the post-sentence interview is passed on to prison-based staff, for example where there is a concern about the possibility of self-harm.

## Social work services in prison

There is no statutory requirement for prison-based social work, but services are provided under a local authority's general duty to promote social welfare (section 12 Social Work (Scotland) Act 1968), in recognition that imprisonment does not remove the right to access general social services. In addition there are specific statutory duties placed on social work (e.g. for the assessment of prisoners who pose a risk to the public and the preparation and provision of reports to the Parole Board) that are easier to fulfil with a presence in prison establishments.

When you consider the social characteristics of prisoners it is clear that they have significant needs that social work services can attempt to address:

> Prisoners are overwhelmingly young, overwhelmingly male and overwhelmingly poor. Statistics issued in 2002 by the Office of the Prime Minister show how depressingly predictable is the population of our prisons ... Compared with the population as a whole, prisoners are fourteen times more likely to have been taken into care as a child, six times more likely to be single teenage parents, five times more likely to have no educational qualification, twelve times more likely to have experienced long-term unemployment, fifty times more likely to suffer from three or more mental disorders, thirty times more likely to be homeless.
>
> (HMCIP, 2002, p. 15)

Research by Houchin (2005) also found clear links between imprisonment and social exclusion, with 28 per cent of the prisoner population coming from the poorest housing estates in Scotland.

Prison social work services are usually delivered by local authority social work departments under contract to the Scottish Prison Service. In the first instance, therefore, the service user is the Prison Service itself, in fulfilment of their sentence management and throughcare responsibilities. The National Standards for throughcare emphasise that there should be a joint commitment on the part of the Scottish Prison Service and local authorities in respect of shared objectives and service outcomes. This is not always easy to maintain within a prison setting where everyday management and security concerns can take priority. The standards therefore maintain that prison officers have a significant role to play in making sure that the social work service in prison is used appropriately and effectively. To that end, penal establishments are required to have systems that ensure that prison officers provide information about the availability of social work services. The theme of partnership is important here, with both social workers and prison officers working towards the same ends – the safety of the public and the successful resettlement of an offender within the community.

Prison social workers work with both short-term and long-term prisoners. A great deal of a prison social worker's time is spent carrying out statutory tasks. They are required to carry out post sentence interviews and risk assessments with anyone sentenced to twelve months or more who is subject to a supervised release order, extended sentence, or life sentence. They also have a duty to see any prisoner who requires social work assistance.

During the course of a prisoner's sentence, the prison social worker will liaise with community-based social workers in relation to home circumstances reports, pre-release work and resettlement. They will also prepare a comprehensive report for consideration by the Parole Board when a prisoner becomes eligible for parole. The prison-based social worker will also be involved in a risk assessment and identifying future work required to attempt to reduce any identified risk.

When an offender is in prison the area-based social worker may be involved with the family, who may experience problems as a result of the imprisonment. It would be expected that the community-based social worker would have been collaborating with the prison-based worker to ensure that the needs of the offender and family were being viewed comprehensively and appropriate responses were being made.

A number of change and development programmes are run in prisons. These programmes usually relate to substance misuse, sexual offending and anger management. They can be delivered jointly by prison officers, social workers and other services and may operate on a group or individual basis. An accreditation scheme by the Scottish Accreditation Panel for Offender Programmes aims to ensure the quality of this work and its potential to reduce reoffending.

Activity 22 asks you to reflect on the role of prison-based social work.

---

Allow about 20 minutes

### Activity 22   Social work services in prison

David, whom you met in Activity 20, has been given a custodial sentence of three years. Make notes in answer to the following questions.

1   What work might you, as a prison-based social worker, do with David?

2   What constraints and opportunities affect the social work role and task in prisons?

### Comment

The objectives of the social work task in prisons have been outlined in the NOS Standards for Throughcare. They are:

- to offer prisoners access to a range and level of social work services similar to those in the community

- to contribute to public safety by making available a range of individual and group work programmes to address offending behaviour

- to provide support and assistance to help prisoners resettle and reintegrate into society following release.

It might be that David could become involved in programmes aimed at anger management and alcohol abuse. Social workers and prison officers might deliver these jointly as part of a strategy of working in partnership. Such groups would tackle offending behaviour by addressing the triggers and problems which led to it and so could help David to settle back into the community on his release with a strategy for coping with the problems which caused his violent behaviour.

Social workers in prison are working within institutions that may have quite different primary objectives, value bases and organisational structures from their own. They will have to work within constraints that may inhibit certain aspects of their practice. Nevertheless, this may be offset by opportunities to develop innovative programmes of work with groups and individuals whose motivation to change may be heightened by the fact of their imprisonment.

### Release, parole and the role of the social worker

The Prisoners and Criminal Proceedings (Scotland) Act 1993 outlines the role of social workers in preparing an offender for release and licence supervision. Social workers have a dual role at this stage, as officers of the Parole Board and advisers to prisoners facing release.

If the offender is made subject to a statutory supervision order or a sentence where they may be released on parole licence, the prison social worker has certain responsibilities. The offender will be seen by the social worker within 21 days of reception into prison. Part of the task of the social worker at this early stage is to engage with the offender in developing a plan for him or her on release. The plan must be achievable. As the release day approaches, the prison social worker will meet with the offender and the community-based social worker who will be responsible for supervision. This meeting should take place about four weeks before the offender's release. When he or she is released into the community, the community-based social worker will take over responsibility for the case.

For long-term sentences, before the Parole Board can consider the case it must have access to a home circumstances report made by a social worker in the area where the prisoner intends to live on release. This report and the report prepared by the prison social worker form part of a dossier compiled for the Parole Board. The dossier may also include reports from psychiatrists, prison psychologists, prison officers and programme workers. The action plan for the offender's release will form part of this dossier.

Statutory supervision, whether the result of a statutory supervision order or a parole licence, has the following objectives:

- to assist offenders to reduce the risk of further offending
- to ensure that offenders released on statutory supervision adhere to their licence conditions
- to facilitate the early release of offenders who are eligible for statutory supervision
- to assist ex-prisoners to reintegrate successfully into the community.

The NOS Standards for Throughcare provide guidelines on supervision in the community, outlining contact requirements and the licence conditions that must be met.

Research into community-based throughcare (McIvor and Barry, 1998) showed that it was viewed as less helpful than it could be by released prisoners and was acknowledged by social work managers to be the least effective of the services funded by central government. There was a difference between the views expressed by social workers and ex-prisoners as to the most significant issues addressed in supervision. Social workers felt that offending behaviour was the most significant issue, while ex-prisoners were most likely to attach importance to accommodation and employment. The problems that caused social workers most difficulty were those related to drug use and finding accommodation for ex-prisoners. The risk of reoffending was increased by problematic alcohol or drug use and general instability in ex-prisoners' lives. It is findings such as these that led to renewed policy attention to the area of throughcare. It remains to be seen, however, whether new initiatives and strategies will result in the delivery of a more effective service.

Activity 23 provides an opportunity to consolidate your understanding of the social worker's role with offenders pre-release.

Allow about 40 minutes     Activity 23   Pre-release work

Imagine that you are a community-based social worker in Paul's case, outlined below, and make notes in answer to the questions that follow.

> Paul was convicted of murder when he was 17. The victim was a gay man from Paul's neighbourhood. Paul knew the victim and he would visit him regularly. The nature of their relationship is unknown. Paul was unemployed at the time of the offence. His friends were in full-time employment. Paul says that he was bored and lonely during the day and would visit the victim with whom he would consume drugs and alcohol. Paul was intoxicated at the time of the offence and says he has no recollection of events.
>
> Paul is now 31. His behaviour in prison has generally been good. Most reports from prison officers are positive, although some state that he can have difficulty in dealing with those in authority. Paul states that some officers are abusive with their power and impose 'silly rules' and they don't like it when he points this out.
>
> Paul has undertaken a great deal of work in prison groups related to cognitive skills, anger management, drug/alcohol misuse and gender. Group leaders are very positive about his participation and development. Paul says that he has learnt a lot from these groups and he is keen to implement what he has learnt in the community. However, he recently failed a drug test. Paul says that this was a 'one off' because he was bored. He added that he is willing to undergo periodic testing to evidence this.
>
> You have met with Paul's parents to prepare a home circumstances report. His parents are extremely supportive of him and are very keen to have him home. They are very disappointed about the positive drug test and clear that they will not tolerate drug misuse. They are both in full-time employment and have arranged employment opportunities for Paul. Paul has taken part in the prison home leave scheme. The family has enjoyed these and there have been no reported incidents in the community. Paul is keen to return home, but says that he will want his own flat eventually.

As part of your home circumstances report you are required to carry out a risk assessment and a resettlement plan for Paul.

I     What risk do you consider Paul presents to the community and what factors influenced your decision?

2     What plan would you present in your report to manage Paul's reintegration into the community and manage any identified risk?

3     Are there any dilemmas or conflicts for you in this situation?

## Comment

In considering risk factors present in Paul's life, it is important to consider factors that were around at the time of the offence, and if any of these remain issues in his life. At the time of his offence drugs and alcohol were factors and he would not appear to have made effective use of his time, that is finding employment or other appropriate daytime activities. Paul has recently failed a drug test and says that his drug misuse was as a result of boredom. These are factors that would give cause for concern. Paul's victim was a gay man, but we are unaware if sexuality was a factor in this offence. Feedback from Paul's participation in the gender group was positive and it would seem sexual identity is perhaps not an issue, although this would have to be checked with Paul and workers who led the group. The possible impact of institutionalisation could also be a factor. Paul has spent most of his adult life in prison. As a result of this, he has not had the same opportunities as his contemporaries in the community to undertake the developmental tasks associated with this age group, for example becoming independent, forming relationships and having his own family. His behaviour in prison can at times seem impetuous and immature, for example drug taking and attitude to those in authority. Paul will be returning to a supportive environment and, given his lack of life experience, it is likely that he will require this support for some time. While Paul is returning to the neighbourhood where his offence was committed, there has been no adverse reaction to his presence in the community.

It could reasonably be expected that any resettlement/risk management plan would focus on the above areas. The social worker may suggest to the Parole Board that additional conditions be added to Paul's licence, for example that he attend drug counselling if directed by his supervising officer, that he can only reside in accommodation approved by his supervising officer, that he attend employment counselling if he has not found employment within three months. These are often standard conditions of a parole licence, but you may wish to ensure that these risks are managed.

The care versus control aspects of this case are likely to present the worker with conflicts and dilemmas. How does a professional commitment to self-determination and choice rest with imposing such strict controls and how do you justify this?

Table 5 summarises the relationship between custodial sentences and the social work role.

### Table 5   Custodial sentences and the social work role

**Short-term**

| *Under 12 months* | *Over 12 months and under 4 years* |
|---|---|
| No order and release at half-way point of sentence. Sex offenders could be subject to an extended sentence and where the sentence is six months to four years will be released on licence. | Release at half-way point. Possibility of court order, i.e. a supervised release order, or in the case of sex offenders an extended sentence. |
| Social work role: Person entitled to voluntary social work assistance at point of sentence, throughout sentence, and for twelve months following release. Sex offenders subject to social work intervention post-sentence and on supervision following release. | Social work role: Person interviewed by social work post-sentence. Possibility of social work intervention throughout sentence. Subject to social work supervision following release (where a relevant order is made). |

**Long-term**

| | |
|---|---|
| *Over 4 years but not life* | *Life sentences* |
| Consideration for parole at half-way point. If unsuccessful, released on non-parole licence at two-thirds point. Violent or sexual offenders may also be subject to an extended sentence. | Mandatory life prisoners considered for parole following consultation with Lord Justice General. Discretionary life and order for lifelong restriction prisoners considered for parole after they have served period stipulated by trial judge at point of sentence. |
| Social work role: Interview post-sentence. Possibility of intervention throughout sentence. Preparation of home circumstances report and parole report for consideration for parole. Also home circumstances report for home leave purposes. Social work supervision on release. | Social work role: Interview post-sentence. Possibility of intervention throughout sentence. Preparation of home circumstances report and parole report for consideration for parole. Also home circumstances report for home leave purposes. Subject to social work supervision for life. |

## 2.8 Supervision and management of offenders in the community

We have seen that a key role for criminal justice social work is the supervision and management of offenders in the community. This includes ex-prisoners under a statutory supervision order or on parole licence, court ordered community disposals and diversion schemes. The supervision role is complex and the requirements are outlined in the conditions attached to each order and the NOS.

Activity 24 is designed to help you to understand the practice issues that arise in relation to community supervision and how the law frames this practice.

Allow about 1 hour

Website

### Activity 24   Understanding probation

We now return to Leo, who you last met in Activity 19 when considering his SER. The decision of the court was that he would be placed on probation for two years with an additional requirement of drug treatment.

Following the links from this activity on the course website, read the Law Resource summary of a probation order's requirements and Chapters 3 and 4 of the National Standards on Probation. Then make notes in answer to the following questions:

1   What is meant by probation?

2   As Leo's social worker, what will be your role?

3   What are the standard conditions that will be attached to Leo's order?

### Comment

The legal basis for probation is the Criminal Procedure (Scotland) Act 1995 (s. 228–234). Probation is an order that requires the offender 'to be under supervision for a period to be specified in the order not less than six months and not more than three years'. A probation order requires that the offender should be of good behaviour and comply with the instructions of the supervising officer. The first Probation of Offenders Act (1907) defined the duties of the supervising officer as being 'to supervise, advise, assist and befriend'.

Leo was in danger of being given a custodial sentence. The National Standards suggest that priority should be given to offenders whose current offending places them at risk of custody and who seem likely to reoffend, or who are repeat offenders with significant problems and who are at risk of custody, even if the current offence is trivial. Leo would seem to fit the first of these categories.

Probation for Leo will accord with the 'twin-track' approach:

- all non-violent offenders except the most serious should be dealt with in the community
- all violent offenders except the less serious may face custody as a means of protecting the public unless appropriate alternatives are available.

It is the role of the court, not the social worker, to explain the effect of probation to Leo and he will be required to express his willingness to comply with the conditions. The social worker would need, however, to have explained probation and checked whether Leo is willing to consent before recommending probation in the SER. As his social worker you will need to meet with Leo within a week of his probation order being made. He will sign the order to show he understands what it means and any conditions contained in it.

The National Standards contain a range of requirements in relation to probation. You will remember that where a probation order is recommended, the SER has to include an action plan that makes it clear what the offender will be required to do and indicates the services which can be made available in order to minimise the risk of reoffending. You will discuss the action plan with Leo and set out specific tasks and responsibilities that you will both undertake to carry out. In drawing up an action plan the victim perspective should be considered and pursued during supervision.

You will also need to clarify how often you and Leo will meet, and where, and explain what may happen if he does not comply with the conditions. Supervising social workers should 'demonstrate a concern to make probation a positive and worthwhile experience and [your] approach should be encouraging, consistent, and practical. Wherever possible the offender's strengths and motivation should be built in' (Scottish Executive, 2004f, para. 60).

The National Standards, however, provide little guidance on best practice in relation to the content of supervision. For example, Leo's personal responsibility for meeting the terms of his probation should always be emphasised. Because of his family's previous contact with social work services he may have different expectations of this role and the social worker should encourage him to take responsibility and guide him in becoming an active participant in the change process. Supervising social workers must always strive to develop a constructive working relationship with the offender and should not promise services (or threaten the use of powers) when they do not intend to deliver. Effective intervention with Leo may include work with him and his mother and will require you, as the social worker, to use the same range of skills that you practise in other forms of social work intervention. You will add to this a specialist knowledge of work in the criminal justice context, but the core skills are transferable.

There are three standard conditions for a probation order:

1 The offender must be of good behaviour.
2 He or she must comply with the instructions given by the supervising officer.
3 The supervising officer must be informed at once of any change of address or employment.

Other formal conditions can be added by the court. However, it is important to distinguish these legal requirements from the working agreements made between the supervising officer and a probationer in the course of an order (McNeill and Whyte, forthcoming).

If an offender placed on probation failed to keep any of the conditions attached to the order they would be in breach of the order. This is an area where a criminal justice social worker would use discretion, guided by agency criteria. They would have to decide on the seriousness of the breach and in the first instance might deal with it by way of a formal written warning. McIvor and Barry (1998) found that 46 per cent of probationers had received one formal warning for non-compliance. For social workers there can be a tension between the needs of the individual and the duty to the court. Fabb and Guthrie emphasise the need for caution in this area:

> Clearly these decisions are not taken lightly since the liberty of an individual is in jeopardy and so it is imperative that there be an internal logic and consistency. This is unfortunately also necessary in view of a history of some social workers' therapeutic optimism and/or over-identification with the service user.
>
> (1997, p. 249)

National Standards require that after two warnings the offender should be reported. However, where a person subject to probation commits another offence there is no discretion: they would automatically be in breach and their supervisor must initiate breach proceedings. The supervising officer has to prepare a report for the court that contains the grounds alleging the breach. It is then up to the court to decide what to do – either the person will be brought to court by way of a warrant implemented by the police or will be sent a letter ordering them to appear. An offender who has breached an order can be fined, the order can be revoked or varied and they can be sentenced for the original offence.

The Management of Offenders etc. (Scotland) Act 2005 further tightens the accountability of probation supervision by providing for probation progress reviews. These can be ordered by the original sentencing court. The social worker must submit a written report on the offender's progress under supervision and the probationer is required to attend. The court has the power to amend the probation order at this stage.

Activity 25 will increase your understanding of the social work role in relation to community service orders.

Allow about 1 hour

### Activity 25   Understanding community service

Website

Following the links from this activity on the course website, read the Law Resource summary of community service orders and Chapters 1 and 5–7 of the National Standards for Community Service. Then make notes in answer to the following questions:

1   What is meant by community service?

2   What is the role of the criminal justice social worker in relation to a community service order?

3   What standard conditions are attached to a community service order?

### Comment

The legal basis for a community service order is the Criminal Procedure (Scotland) Act 1995 (s. 238–245). Community service orders require the offender to undertake unpaid work for the benefit of the community as an alternative to a custodial sentence. They can only be made with the consent of the offender and after an SER has been received from a social worker which comments on the person's suitability to undertake such an order and the availability of an appropriate placement. The National Standards for Community Service explain that risk assessment is necessary to assess the suitability of an offender for community service, informed by their previous offending history, the nature of the placement, the degree of supervision to be given and the vulnerability of the recipient. The local authority officer should also take into account the skills and interests of the offender and involve them in the decision making about an appropriate placement (Scottish Executive, 2004g). In addition under section 293(3) of the Criminal Procedure (Scotland Act) 1995 instructions given for unpaid work should as far as is practical 'avoid conflict with the offender's religious beliefs, and any interference with the time, if any, at which he normally works or attends school or other educational establishment'.

Criminal justice social workers are often not involved in direct work with offenders on their placement in the community. In this way community service orders differ from probation. Community service orders also do not focus directly on addressing the offending behaviour and may not provide the opportunities for one-to-one work that are possible within the probation relationship. Local authorities are responsible for the administration of community service placements and this role may be performed by a criminal justice social worker or a community service officer who is employed by the local authority and who may not have a social work qualification. The officer's role is primarily one of supervision and enforcement; they monitor the offender's compliance with the requirements of a community service order.

The standard conditions attached to a community service order are that an offender must report for work when required to do so and report any change of address or employment. They should also normally complete their order within a 12-month period. The only grounds for initiating breach procedures for a community service order are failing to meet one or more of these requirements or failing to perform the work satisfactorily. The NOS outline the disciplinary procedures to be followed in case of breach but, as with a probation order, there is a degree of professional discretion given to the supervising officer. However, in contrast to probation, the commission of a further offence does not automatically constitute a breach of a community service order (although it may lead to the order being breached on other grounds).

## Supervising sex offenders

A particular source of public anxiety in recent years has been the supervision of sex offenders in the community. As we have seen, sex offenders who are sent to custody are all subject to post-release supervision, some for an extended period. The Sex Offenders Act 1997 required persons convicted of certain sex offences to register their name and address with the police and to keep the police notified of any changes for a set period of years, depending on the original sentence. They may also be issued with a sexual offence prevention order (under the Crime and Disorder Act 1998), a civil order that can prohibit any conduct in order to protect the public, breach of which is a criminal offence. The notification requirements have been strengthened in recent years and are now found in the Sexual Offences Act 2003. Arrangements for supervision have been tightened by the introduction of public protection arrangements in the Management of Offenders etc. (Scotland) Act 2005, and a new police led violent and sex offenders register (VISOR) system is due to be adopted across Scotland. Social workers now have a duty to work alongside the police, housing authorities and other relevant bodies (i.e. schools and childcare services) in making multi-agency public protection arrangements (MAPPAs) which are coordinated by each CJA. Box 19 explains the role of MAPPAs in more detail.

**Box 19 Multi-agency public protection arrangements (MAPPAs)**

The police, local authorities, Scottish Prison Service and the NHS (for mentally disordered offenders) have a statutory duty to establish joint arrangements to assess and manage the risk posed by sexual and violent offenders.

MAPPAs operate on four principles of good practice:
- defensible decisions
- rigorous risk assessment
- delivering risk management plans matching identified public protection needs
- evaluation of performance to improve delivery.

They have four core functions:
- identifying MAPPA offenders
- sharing relevant information
- assessing the risk of serious harm
- managing that risk.

(Adapted from Scottish Executive, 2006b, p. 18)

Criminal justice social work should be planned and organised to provide a portfolio of services for sex offenders, including supervision, advice and assistance, and work with offenders on personal change (SWSI, 1997). This will include:

- drawing up a supervision plan which is based on an assessment of the offender, the risk he or she poses, and what steps can be taken to reduce the risk of reoffending

- providing advice and assistance so that the offender is able to change those circumstances which are related to his or her risk of reoffending, for example by getting a job, developing appropriate adult relationships

- where there is a high level of risk, providing intensive supervision.

In addition further steps might be taken, depending on the circumstances. These include:

- requiring the offender to keep a diary
- electronic monitoring
- frequent home visits
- telephone contact
- obtaining a 'second report' by recruiting someone who knows the offender to report on them
- periodic intensive assessment and reviews
- spot checks
- interrogative supervision, that is, a more probing supervisory encounter.

The purpose of supervision in this area is the overseeing of offenders and the assessment, management and reduction of risk. Though this may sound relatively straightforward, the challenge of working effectively with sex offenders should not be underestimated, not least because of the political, cultural, personal and value tensions that surround this highly charged area of professional practice. As with all areas of social work practice, the challenge for practitioners is to remain open, informed, reflective and critical in relation to both their own practice and those they will inevitably work alongside.

In many respects, the expectations of supervision detailed above are broadly the same as they would be for any offender subject to social work supervision. The emphasis on risk assessment and the expectation that intervention or supervision plans will be informed by valid, reliable and ongoing assessment, affects all areas of criminal justice social work. In addition, social workers are expected to make critical use of the extensive body of research now emerging in this area and the many assessment tools and change programmes now available (see Levy et al., 2002).

## Risk management and effective practice

As the task of managing risk and reducing reoffending has moved to the fore, there has been much research into what constitutes effective work to reduce reoffending with offenders. This has become known as the 'what works?' research, which seeks to identify the types and components of programmes that are most consistently associated with positive outcomes in reducing reoffending (Andrews et al., 1990; Lipsey, 1990). These features were collated into six key principles by McGuire and Priestley in 1995 and have since been widely published and disseminated in this form across the UK. The six key principles identified by McGuire and Priestley are outlined in Box 20.

---

**Box 20 The 'what works?' research**

*1 The risk principle*
Intervention is most effective when the level of supervision matches the individual's risk of reoffending.

*2 The need principle*
The content of intervention should be designed to effectively address those problems and needs which are related, either directly or indirectly, to an individual's offending. These needs are known as 'criminogenic' needs (i.e. crime supporting needs).

*3 The responsivity principle*
The most effective styles and modes of intervention are those systematically matched with the needs, circumstances and learning styles of the individual.

Research identifies 'general' and 'specific' responsivity considerations:

- *General responsivity considerations:* generally the most effective styles and modes of service are structured and active ones such as social learning and cognitive behavioural approaches, as opposed to reliance upon evocative, relationship-dependent, self-reflective, verbally interactive and insight-orientated approaches

- *Specific responsivity considerations*: intervention must respond to factors including gender, age, intelligence, interpersonal skills and ethnicity, etc.

*4 Community base*

Programmes located in the community, on balance, yield more effective outcomes.

*5 Treatment modality*

Effective interventions use a variety of approaches and methods to address criminogenic needs.

*6 Programme integrity*

Interventions should be rigorously managed and delivered as designed.

(McGuire and Priestley, 1995, pp. 14–15)

In addition to these key principles, McGuire and Priestley identify that amongst the range of intervention methods included, those which emerge as offering the most promising outcomes are based on the 'cognitive behavioural' approach. This engages offenders in improving their thinking skills on the assumption that unacceptable behaviour is caused by distortions in the way offenders think about their crimes.

The 'what works?' research has had a considerable impact upon practice. The last decade has seen the increasing use of standardised risk assessment tools within agencies across Scotland, the development of national accreditation panels – designed to ensure the development and delivery of community supervision programmes that accord with the 'what works?' principles – and, perhaps most significantly, the increasing adoption of structured, cognitive behavioural, offence-focused programmes.

On the whole the above developments have been welcomed in so far as they contribute to a more evidence-based approach to intervention with offenders. However, in taking these messages forward into practice, it is important to give brief attention to some of the perceived limitations of the ' what works?' research. The most common criticisms surrounding the research fall into two main areas:

- 'Programmes over people' – a number of critics have argued that recent preoccupations with the development and delivery of structured, cognitive behavioural programmes have resulted in a neglect of the importance of the 'people' involved in supervision. For example, attention to individual needs and the importance of the development of a constructive working relationship between supervisor and offender can be overlooked.

- The neglect of 'the social' – other commentators suggest that the focus on cognitive behavioural programmes – a method recognised for its focus on the individual offender and on the modification of his or her thoughts, attitudes, reasoning and problem-solving skills – has resulted in a neglect of the broader social circumstances known to be associated with offending behaviour. This runs contrary to social work values:

> Cognitive-behavioural interventions with offenders are rarely conducive to the development of practice that is aimed at empowerment, enhancing social justice and promoting inclusion in society.
>
> (McIvor, 2004, p. 308)

Perhaps in response to these criticisms recent research has seen a renewed attention to the broader processes required to support change and in particular places emphasis not just on 'what' is done with the offender, but 'how' that is done. As McNeill et al. (2005) conclude in a recent review of the core skills required for effective criminal justice social work practice:

> Offenders under supervision have very high levels of need. Moreover, although most offenders have many needs in common, there are also significant variations that necessitate the thoughtful tailoring of individual interventions if the effectiveness of practice is to be maximised. In delivering effective practice, the accumulated weight of evidence ... drives us towards recognition that practice skills in general and relationship skills in particular are at least as critical in reducing re-offending as programme content.
>
> (McNeill et al., 2005, p. 5)

The above research raises, then, many challenges to social workers concerned to practise ethically and effectively in the current policy climate. However, when applied critically and reflectively, emerging knowledge about 'what works?' presents a very real opportunity for social work to demonstrate its effectiveness in achieving positive outcomes that are in the interest of the public, the victims of offending and offenders themselves.

## 2.9 Conclusion

It is evident that while the law is very important in framing social work practice in the criminal justice process, social work skills and values are central to effective interventions.

The social work role in the adult criminal justice system is both demanding and rewarding. As crime has become increasingly prominent on the political and public agenda, so social work's role in the criminal justice system has become more prominent and more complex. This section traced the core responsibilities of the social worker in the criminal justice system, which include:

- writing SERs that have a positive impact on sentencing practice
- working within the prison and supervising community throughcare orders, again, with a view to reducing reoffending
- supervising community disposals, for example probation, in such a way as to have a positive impact on reoffending rates.

Within each of these areas it has been apparent that social workers have a professional responsibility towards a range of stakeholders involved in the criminal justice process, including the victims of crime, the court, the community and offenders themselves. In order to fulfil this role effectively, social workers need to have a clear and confident understanding of their role and task, an understanding of the legislative and policy context informing that role, and a commitment to developing the knowledge, skills and values required for effective and ethical practice.

In the next section we look at children, young people and criminal justice.

## Key points

- The social worker has an important role at key stages in the criminal justice process to divert offenders from prosecution and custody and to prevent reoffending.
- Social workers provide information to the procurator fiscal, the court and the Parole Board to assist their decision making.
- They have an important role in the assessment of offenders and risk management.
- They supervise offenders subject to community disposals, statutory supervision orders and parole.
- Social workers are responsible for writing SERs. This is a complex task and these reports can influence the sentence received by the offender.
- Social workers in prison collaborate with community-based social workers to try to make sure that the needs of the offender and their family are met.

# 3 Children, young people and criminal justice

For this section you will need:
- course website access for online activities
- Children (Scotland) Act 1995 wall chart.

## Core questions

- How does the legal system respond to children and young people who break the criminal law?
- What is the age of criminal responsibility in Scotland?
- What is the relationship between the children's hearings system and the criminal justice process?
- What is the social work role in youth justice?
- How have policy developments impacted on this role?

## 3.1 Introduction

Scotland's legal response to children and young people who offend has long been regarded as distinctive. It is commended for adopting a primarily welfare-based approach that engages two different systems (children's hearings and criminal justice) in the pursuit of 'youth justice'. For social workers in this field – whether working with children and families, or as criminal justice social workers working with young people in the adult criminal justice process – the relationship between these two systems can be difficult to understand and negotiate. The public, as service users and people who are concerned about the harm that children and young people may inflict, are also often ill informed about the process of youth justice in Scotland (NCH Scotland, 2004). This section therefore provides an overview of the law in this area and considers how it frames social work practice.

This section also introduces recent policy developments in relation to antisocial behaviour and persistent offenders, which commentators have suggested mark a move away from the Kilbrandon philosophy towards increased criminal justice intervention into the lives of children and young people and a more punitive response (e.g. McAra, 2006; Piacentini and Walters, 2006). Youth offending is an area that attracts a high level of public and political scrutiny and since devolution Scottish youth justice policy and practice have been subject to extensive review and reform. At the time of writing the Scottish Executive is undertaking a review of the children's hearings system that is likely to lead to further legislative change (Scottish Executive, 2006d). You will be asked to reflect on the implications of this policy context for effective and ethical social work and to consider how an understanding of legal issues such as children's rights can assist in the promotion of social work values.

We will start by taking a closer look at youth crime, the 'problem' that the law in this area seeks to address.

## 3.2 Youth crime and criminalisation

Children and young people are responsible for a significant amount of reported crime in Scotland. Given that the under-21s make up less than one-fifth of the population they contribute disproportionately to the crime figures, accounting for over 40 per cent of certain types of crime (e.g. housebreaking, vandalism and theft of motor vehicles) (Audit Scotland, 2001). This is consistent with criminological research that suggests that offending behaviour is relatively 'normal' for young people, particularly young males, many of whom engage in minor criminal activity and have transient contact with the police before 'growing-out' of crime. The peak ages of offending in Scotland (18 years for males, 15 for females) also reflect this trend. Not all youth offending, however, can be viewed as 'normal'. It is now widely accepted that a small number of persistent offenders account for a high proportion of all offences and responding to their behaviour is more problematic (McNeill and Batchelor, 2004) (see also Activity 33 below).

The following factors have been associated with a risk of offending by young people:

- gender – with boys more likely to offend than girls
- family factors, including poor parental supervision, harsh and inconsistent discipline, parental conflict and parental rejection
- growing up in poor neighbourhoods
- educational problems, including poor school attendance, attainment and truancy
- abusing alcohol or drugs
- criminal associations, e.g. peer group pressure and criminality.

Generally, studies confirm the significant implications of early criminal activity and antisocial behaviour, family disruption and poor educational attainment. While children exposed to the above risk factors are more likely to end up as serious or persistent offenders, it is clear that these are not automatic predictors and many will not go on to become offenders, or if they do, will not continue their activity into adulthood. Research has also identified the following 'resilience' factors that may assist children to survive risky experiences, including:

- their individual characteristics, e.g. having a resilient temperament or positive social orientation
- positive relationships with family members, teachers or other adults
- close friendship with peers.

These research findings are summarised in a review of effective interventions with children and young people involved in crime, which concluded that community-based programmes that address these complex individual and social needs can 'work' to prevent and reduce offending (Whyte, 2005).

Serious harm caused by children and young people remains rare, but often these cases are very influential in determining the strategies devised to respond to young people who offend. For example, the 1993 murder of 2-year-old James Bulger by two 10-year-old boys in England arguably resulted in a hardening of public attitudes across the UK. More recently, concern about antisocial behaviour and persistent offending has shaped the political agenda in Scotland and led to the introduction of increasingly punitive responses. There has been a shift from a holistic child welfare focus to a concern to protect victims and communities from crime in a way that commentators suggest may exaggerate the actual risks posed. Research into public attitudes towards young people and youth crime in Scotland shows a widespread belief that the amount of crime committed by young people is higher than a decade ago, despite evidence to the contrary (Anderson et al., 2005). Lesley McAra claims there is a 'full-blown moral panic' about youth offending that exploits public fears and could have serious repercussions for effective interventions with young people:

> this is a strategy which risks the further exclusion and alienation of young people from the neighbourhoods within which they live, with damaging consequences in terms of both community cohesion and the more inclusive and nurturing elements of the youth justice policy frame.
>
> (McAra, 2006, p. 142)

Appearances can be deceptive

It is important to recognise, therefore, that the response to youth crime may actually contribute to the 'problem'. The demonisation and criminalisation of youth and youth culture, through, for example, the labelling of 'neds' and the banning of 'hoodies', tells us both about the experiences of children and young people in Scotland today and also about the communities in which they live. Public attitudes and perceptions in this area are not simply a reflection of young people's behaviour; they may also help constitute the problem (Anderson et al., 2005). An example of this can be seen in the recent policy focus on antisocial behaviour by young people. Box 21 outlines two relevant legal provisions.

---

### Box 21  Antisocial behaviour orders and the dispersal of groups

Section 4 of the Antisocial Behaviour etc. (Scotland) Act 2004 extends the use of antisocial behaviour orders (ASBOs) to individuals aged 12 years or older (previously the use of ASBOs was limited in Scotland to those aged 16 or over). ASBOs are a civil order (where the evidence is assessed on the balance of probabilities) prohibiting conduct for the purpose of protecting persons from further antisocial behaviour. They can be issued by the sheriff court on application by the local authority or a registered social landlord. Before granting an order on someone under 16, a children's hearing will be held and the sheriff will consider the advice of the principal reporter to the children's hearing before making the decision whether to grant a full ASBO. Breach of this order is a criminal offence, with a statutory power of arrest, and will result in a referral to the procurator fiscal.

Section 19 of the Antisocial Behaviour etc. (Scotland) Act 2004 creates a new power for a senior police officer to designate an area, in consultation with the local authority, where significant, persistent and serious antisocial behaviour has occurred and the presence or behaviour of groups is contributing to the problems. In the designated area the police will have the power to disperse groups of two or more people or individuals within groups where their presence or behaviour is causing, or is likely to cause, alarm or distress to any member of the public. In deciding whether to use that power the constable has to be satisfied that by doing so the alarm and distress is likely to lessen. The police can require any person who does not live in the area to leave, and can also prohibit them from returning to the area for the next 24 hours. It is not an offence to be given a direction to disperse from the police, but if individuals refuse to abide by the constable's direction they will be committing an offence. In these circumstances, police can arrest without warrant.

Further information and guidance on the Scottish Executive's antisocial behaviour strategy can be found on the Antisocial Behaviour website listed in the course Directory.

---

Activity 26 asks you to consider these provisions and their possible implications for the policing of young people.

Website

Allow about 25 minutes

## Activity 26   Young people and antisocial behaviour

Following the link from this activity on the course website, read the Law Resource summary of antisocial behaviour orders. Using this and the information provided on ASBOs and dispersal orders in Box 21, write notes in answer to the following questions:

1   What is antisocial behaviour?

2   Is antisocial behaviour a crime?

3    Do you have the right to walk in a public place in a group of two or more people?

4    What implications could these legal provisions have for young people, their relationships within their community and with the police?

## Comment

Section 143(1) of the Antisocial Behaviour etc. (Scotland) Act defines antisocial behaviour as 'acting in a manner that causes or is likely to cause alarm or distress', or 'pursuing a course of conduct that causes or is likely to cause alarm or distress to at least one person who is not of the same household'. This is an extremely wide definition that encompasses behaviour ranging from vandalism and assault, to minor 'incivilities' that are otherwise legal, such as swearing and hanging around in public places. The expressed intention behind this legislation was to provide communities with stronger measures to deal with the kind of behaviour that 'blights lives', which existing legal measures had failed to prevent (Scottish Executive 2004h). It has, however, attracted controversy:

> While few dispute that there is a 'problem' of antisocial behaviour, it is a socially constructed term, and the use of ASBOs can criminalise young people ... as well as being exclusive. They signal the criminalisation of social policy and also, argues Brown (2004), blur the boundaries between criminal and other forms of social control.
>
> (Croall, 2005, p. 193)

This is because what constitutes antisocial behaviour is largely in the eye of the beholder, and can be affected by negative attitudes towards and fear of young people. Although this legislation is not directly targeted at youth, they are one of the groups most vulnerable to the policing of its provisions (along with social housing tenants and the mentally disordered). ASBOs and dispersal powers therefore potentially widen the 'net' of youth justice. While they are not in themselves criminal orders, their use can accelerate the contact between young people and the formal legal process, bringing them into direct confrontation with the police and criminalising disobedience. Research from the Edinburgh Study into Youth Transitions and Crime suggests that certain categories of young people are particularly at risk of unfair targeting and adversarial police contact. Categories of suspiciousness were found to be class related, with distinctions made between 'respectable' and 'unrespectable' children that were not supported by actual levels of offending (McAra and McVie, 2005).

Social workers committed to anti-discriminatory practice should note the potential for legislative initiatives and the exercise of legal powers to further marginalise vulnerable groups. Research suggests that social workers and children's services have a pivotal role to play in deciding when ASBOs are sought for young people, and to date their use has been rare in Scotland. Executive guidance maintains that ASBOs should be used as a last resort for children under the age of 16, where other options have failed (Scottish Executive, 2006e). However, current policy encourages local authorities to make full use of their powers in this area.

It is important to recognise that both crime and crime control practices have a particular impact on children and young people. As well as being perpetrators of crime, it is less readily acknowledged that children and young people are disproportionately its victims. They are also less likely to have recourse to the protection of the justice system, for example because they may not recognise or report offending behaviour and, historically at least, have not always been treated as credible witnesses in court. Social workers have a role in addressing these inequalities by, for example, providing advice and support to vulnerable witnesses and children who are referred to social work services.

You may recall from Section 1 of this block that professionals within the legal system (e.g. the police, procurators fiscal and social workers) have a crucial role to play in constructing the reaction to children and young people through the exercise of their discretion to police, to prosecute or intervene in children's (and their families) lives. This discretion is, however, vulnerable to swings in public policy in relation to youth crime and changing philosophies of youth 'justice', which provides a challenging environment for social work practice. Nevertheless, it remains the case that the majority of children who commit offences in Scotland do not come before the criminal courts and many are not even referred to a children's hearing. This is in line with research evidence that formal legal responses can exacerbate offending behaviour and that informal problem-based interventions which divert children and young people away from the criminal justice process are more likely to address the complex causes of youth crime and social disadvantage (NCH Scotland, 2004).

## 3.3 Children's rights and criminal responsibility

There is something of a paradox at the heart of Scotland's approach to children and young people who commit criminal offences. On the one hand the legal process aims to protect them from the full rigour of the criminal justice system, while on the other hand it has one of the lowest ages of criminal responsibility in the world (8 years old). The age at which children assume legal responsibility for their actions varies according to context, perceptions of their capacity, and historical and cultural definitions of 'childhood'. Table 6 allows you to compare the age of criminal responsibility in other countries.

**Table 6   Age of criminal responsibility in other European countries**

| | |
|---|---|
| Belgium | 18 |
| England and Wales | 10 |
| France | 13 |
| Ireland | 12 |
| Norway | 15 |
| Scotland | 8 |
| Spain | 16 |

Commentators have observed that the low age of criminal responsibility in Scotland is 'slightly out of kilter' with the Kilbrandon philosophy and has a symbolic significance that can contribute to pressure for the further 'responsibilization' and punishment of children (McAra, 2006, p. 137). The Scottish Law Commission and the Scottish Executive's own review of youth crime have both recommended raising the age of criminal capacity to 12 years (Scottish Law Commission, 2002; Scottish Executive, 2000), but action has yet to be taken. In 2002 the United Nations Committee on the Rights of the Child also recommended that the UK should considerably raise the minimum age of criminal responsibility in order to become compliant with its obligations in international law under the United Nations Convention on the Rights of the Child (UNCRC).

The Kilbrandon Committee itself did not suggest changing the age of criminal responsibility on the basis that most children under the age of 16 would not come before the criminal courts. But we will see from the next section that Scotland retains the ability to try children accused of certain categories of crime in the adult criminal justice process and this raises significant issues for children's rights. Box 22 summarises key provisions of the UNCRC as they relate to 'juvenile' justice. As this document is not directly enforceable in Scots domestic law, incompatibility with the UNCRC cannot form the basis of a legal challenge, but social workers have a value commitment to protect the rights and interests of service users and to respect such international conventions.

**Box 22 The UNCRC and youth justice**

The convention applies to every human being below the age of 18 (Article 1).

The key principles are:

- All of the convention rights are guaranteed without discrimination (Article 2).
- The best interests of the child must be a primary consideration in all actions concerning children (Article 3).
- That children's views must be considered and taken into account in all matters affecting them (Article 12).

The specific provisions include:

- No child shall be subjected to torture or other cruel, inhuman or degrading treatment or punishment. Neither capital punishment nor life imprisonment without possibility of release shall be imposed for offences committed by persons below 18 years of age (Article 37(a)).
- The arrest, detention or imprisonment of a child shall be used only as a measure of last resort and for the shortest appropriate period of time (Article 37(b)).
- Every child deprived of liberty shall be treated in a manner that takes into account the needs of persons of his or her age. In particular they should be separated from adults unless it is considered in this child's best interests not to do so (Article 37(c)).
- Every child deprived of liberty has the right to access legal and other appropriate assistance and to challenge the legality of their detention before a court or other independent, impartial authority (Article 37(d)).
- Every child alleged as, accused of, or recognized as having infringed the penal law is to be treated in a manner consistent with the promotion of the child's sense of dignity and worth, which reinforces the child's respect for the human rights and fundamental freedoms of others and which takes into account the child's age and the desirability of promoting the child's reintegration and the child's assuming a constructive role in society (Article 40 (1)).
- To this end certain due process rights, including prompt determination of their case and the right to privacy at all stages of the proceedings, are guaranteed (Article 40 (2)).

State parties shall seek to establish:

- a separate youth justice system specifically for children (Article 40(3)), and

- a minimum age of criminal responsibility (Article 40(3)(a)), and
- provide measures for dealing with children who offend without resorting to judicial proceedings, as long as rights and legal safeguards are respected (Article 40(3)(b), and

- provide alternatives to institutional care to ensure that children are dealt with in a manner appropriate to their well-being and proportionate to both their circumstances and the offence (Article 40(4)).

These provisions will be referred to throughout this section in order to assess the current legal arrangements and consider their implications for social work practice. First you need to understand the relationship between the children's hearings system and the criminal justice process in Scotland.

## 3.4 Understanding the two-system approach

Figure 10 provides an overview of the legal process that applies to children and young people who are suspected of committing a crime. This is an important reference source and you will find it useful to copy this to refer back to during your work on this section.

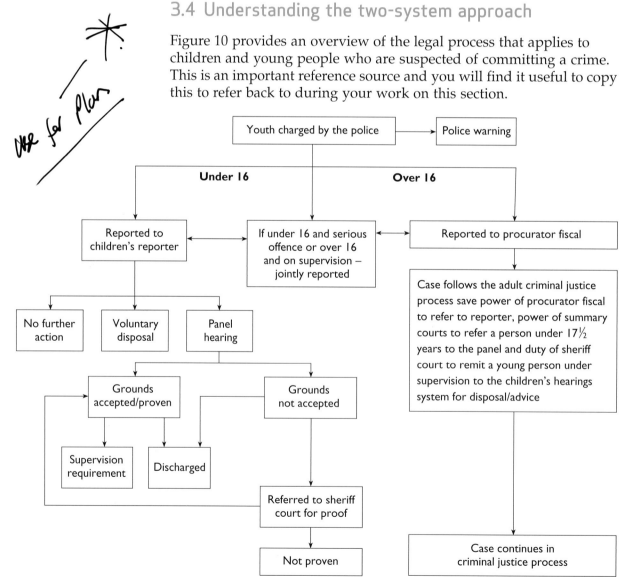

Figure 10    Flow diagram of youth justice processes

Figure 10 covers the period from police charge to the disposal of the case and outlines the relationship between the children's hearings system and the criminal justice process. Activity 27 helps you to make sense of this diagram and the parallel legal processes that children and young people may encounter.

Allow about 40 minutes **Activity 27   The children's hearings system and the criminal justice process.**

Wall charts

Examine Figure 10, the flow diagram of youth justice processes, and the Children (Scotland) Act 1995 wall chart, taking particular note of the 'principles applicable generally to orders involving children' and the boxes on the children's hearings system. Use these resources to inform your answers to the following questions:

1   Is there a separate youth justice process in Scotland?

2   What is the relevance of age to the route that a case will follow?

3   Can children and young people enter the adult criminal justice process?

4   What happens when the person referred to a children's hearing disputes the grounds of their referral (i.e. claims that they have not committed an offence)?

5   What are the key legal principles that apply in the children's hearings system?

## Comment

Despite the use of the term in policy documents there is no separate youth justice process in Scotland. Instead, there are two very different legal systems that operate in parallel: the children's hearings system and the 'adult' criminal justice process. The children's hearing system is an integrated response to both children in need of care or protection and those who offend, based on the fact that the two groups are considered to have much in common, specifically that the roots of their difficulties often stem from similar experience of social and/or emotional disadvantage. The focus is on the child's best interests and not punishment.

The age of a child or young person is relevant to the legal framework that governs their case, for example children under the age of 8 cannot be charged by the police or referred to the reporter on an offence ground. However, the age of the accused is not the only factor that will be considered. In Scotland a child of 8 can be dealt with in the criminal justice system, although there are strict guidelines governing such decisions. Section 42 (1) of the Criminal Procedure (Scotland) Act 1995 states that 'no child under the age of 16 years shall be prosecuted for any offence except on the instructions of the Lord Advocate ... and no court other than the High Court and the sheriff court shall have jurisdiction over a child under the age of 16 years for an offence'. Guidelines are issued by the Lord Advocate to chief constables about the offences for which a child can be prosecuted (COPFS, 2006). These are summarised in Box 23.

**Box 23 Lord Advocate's Guidelines on the reporting of children**

The following categories of offences must be reported to the procurator fiscal:

• serious offences which are required by law to be prosecuted on indictment and normally give rise to solemn proceedings (such as murder and rape)

• offences alleged to have been committed by children aged 15 years or over that in the event of conviction oblige or permit a court to order disqualification from driving (excluding minor road traffic offences)

- offences alleged to have been committed by children aged 16–17 years who are currently the subject of a supervision order in the children's hearings system
- breaches of ASBOs allegedly committed by children aged 12–15 years only if they are accompanied by other serious offending behaviour.

When reporting to the procurators fiscal cases against adults in which it is alleged that a child also committed an offence, the police should not include the child offender as a subject in the police report, but should state that a copy has been sent to the reporter for action in respect of the child.

Where a child is charged in the circumstances given in Box 23, the case will be 'jointly reported'. This means a report will go from the police to both the reporter and the procurator fiscal, who will liaise over the outcome. There is, therefore, clearly some overlap between the two processes and children and young people can enter the 'adult' criminal justice process.

It is not the role of a children's hearing to determine the guilt or otherwise of the person before them. Where a person is referred by the reporter on an offence ground and this is disputed by the child, the panel may make an application to the sheriff, who will hear the case in private and establish proof according to the criminal standard ('beyond reasonable doubt'). This is in order to protect the rights of the child from intervention on inappropriate grounds and is important because the acceptance of an offence ground in the children's hearing system counts as a criminal offence for the purposes of the Rehabilitation of Offender's Act 1974 (which governs the disclosure of previous convictions). Therefore in these cases the determination of an offence and eventual disposal are split between the criminal courts and the children's hearings function.

Finally, it is important to remember that the children's hearings function is governed by the legal framework in the Children (Scotland) Act 1995, as described in Block 2, where certain fundamental principles apply. The paramountcy of the welfare principle is, however, qualified by section 16(5) of the Act , which states that courts and hearings can make decisions that are not in the best interests of the child in order to protect others. The protection of the public can therefore take priority in cases referred on offence grounds.

You may have noticed that in certain respects the current legal arrangements in Scotland are not fully compliant with the UNCRC, which for example recommends the establishment of a separate youth justice system for all children under the age of 18 and that the welfare of the child should be the primary consideration in all cases involving children. In many ways, however, the Scottish approach to youth justice, with its emphasis on diversion from prosecution and punishment through the children's hearings system, better respects the child's age, dignity and self worth as required by Article 40 of the UNCRC than countries where children are subject to a separate youth justice process (such as England and Wales).

Activity 28 helps you to think through:
- the process by which a decision is reached about a young person who is accused of having committed an offence
- the social work role in relation to this process.

Allow about 30 minutes    ## Activity 28   Working with Tony

Imagine that you are a social worker involved with the young person in the following scenario. Read Tony's story and using Figure 10, the flow diagram of youth justice processes, make notes in answer to the questions below.

> Tony is 15 years old and was arrested a couple of weeks ago for stealing and driving away a car. He has been in trouble with the police before for a similar offence. When he was 14 years old Tony was caught trying to break into a vehicle with a group of other boys. On that occasion he was given a police warning. He is awaiting a decision on what is going to happen next in the present case.

1   What do you think Tony's main worries are?

2   What do you think he needs to know in order to help him understand what might happen to him?

### Comment

It is likely that Tony's main concern will be whether or not he will have to go to court, and if he does, whether he will get a custodial sentence.

He may not know about the other possible outcomes and so will need information about the process by which a decision will be reached as well as the possible range of sentences which can be imposed by the court (if indeed he goes to court). Where a child is charged with an offence and the report has been made by the police, the procurator fiscal and the reporter will usually liaise to decide which system should deal with the child. The best interests of the child are a factor that will be considered by both of them, but other factors will contribute to the final decision. The procurator fiscal must reach his or her decision having due regard to the public interest, and the gravity of the offence will obviously play a part. Even if the procurator fiscal does decide to proceed with a case, it could still fail to go ahead if there is a lack of sufficient evidence.

Should the decision be that the reporter will deal with the referral (a likely outcome given Tony's age), he or she will follow the procedure of investigation set out in the Children (Scotland) Act 1995. It should be noted that even though a child has been charged with an offence, the reporter may still take no action, if there appears to be no need for compulsory measures of supervision. Even if the reporter decides to put the case to a hearing, the reporter does not have to use the 'offence' ground if there is another ground for referral. This can be important, since an acceptance or finding of guilt counts as a criminal conviction.

In Tony's case the procurator fiscal may decide to keep the case because the disposals available to the hearing are limited. For example, because this is a car-related offence, if he is found guilty then disqualification from driving may be considered an appropriate sentence (the disqualification could take him beyond his 17th birthday).

If his case is dealt with in the criminal process Tony should be made aware that he could be subject to a broad range of sentences, most of which are also available to adult offenders (see Table 3 in Section 2.5 above and information on special disposals available for children and young people in Section 3.7 below). Therefore the worst-case scenario would be that he could lose his liberty by being sentenced to 'detention', although this is highly improbable on the facts of his case.

Social workers have an important role to play with all young people who are in trouble with the police, whether in their capacity as children and families workers or criminal justice social work professionals. For those young people whose involvement with offending is minor and short term, the focus of current policy in on diversion. For those young people who are involved in or at risk of persistent offending, the focus of social work intervention is on preventative strategies, diversion and the provision of effective responses.

Local authority social workers have a responsibility to safeguard the best interests of children and young people who are engaged in the legal process, but this role is complicated by the involvement of two different systems and the division of areas of social work practice (e.g. into children and family services, and criminal justice social work). There is obviously a need for partnership working in the youth justice context across social work specialisms, both within the local authority (e.g. liaison with community warden teams and antisocial behaviour coordinators) and with other agencies and service providers (Youth Justice Improvement Group, 2006). This is far from straightforward, however, because of striking differences in organisational arrangements and objectives.

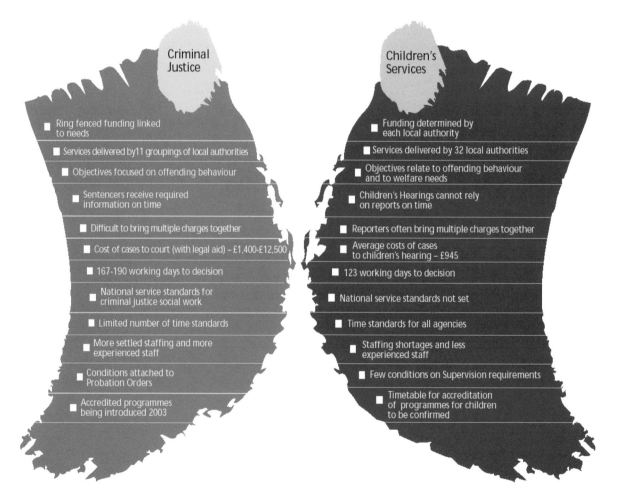

Figure 11    Difference between children's and adult services (Audit Scotland, 2002, p. 27)

Figure 11 illustrates the differences that existed between two key areas of social work responsibility, children's and adult services, before the Scottish Executive embarked on its programme of criminal justice and youth justice reform. We have seen (from Section 1 of this block) that the legal framework in relation to criminal justice social work has recently been strengthened in response to policy demands (through, for example, the tightening of National Standards and the introduction of criminal justice authorities (CJAs)). At the same time children's services in relation to youth justice have also been subject to reform in an attempt to import some of the strengths of the adult system (such as national standards, better funding streams and the accreditation of programmes designed to tackle youth crime) into the children's hearings system.

In 2002 the Scottish Executive launched a ten-point Action Plan on Youth Crime and made a clear commitment to address what were perceived to be the weaknesses of the criminal justice process and the children's hearings system. This included concern over the time taken for referrals and decision making in relation to children and young people, the quality of disposals available and a lack of coordination of 'youth justice' services. This ongoing reform programme has prompted legislative and organisational change across adult and children's services and the piloting of initiatives such as fast-track hearings and youth courts for persistent offenders (see Section 3.6 below). The executive has set a target for a 10 per cent reduction in the number of persistent young offenders by 2008, which presents a significant challenge for social work and other youth justice professions.

A new guidance framework – the National Standards for Youth Justice Services – outlining the objectives and standards to be met in this area, was published in 2002 and all of the relevant partners in youth justice were expected to be compliant by 2006. Like the National Objectives and Standards for Social Work Services in the Criminal Justice System, these do not have force of law, but are reinforced by the accountability frameworks for assessing the quality of social work and other services, and are therefore part of the wider mandate for social work practice in this area.

---

**Box 24 The objectives of youth justice services**

1  To improve the quality of the youth justice process
2  To improve the range and availability of programmes to stop youth offending
3  To reduce the time taken from the initial report on the offender (usually by the police) to the implementation of a hearing decision
4  To improve the information provided to victims and local communities
5  To ensure that secure accommodation is used when it is the most appropriate disposal and ensure it is effective in reducing offending behaviour
6  To improve the strategic direction and co-ordination of youth justice services by local youth justice strategy teams.

(Scottish Executive, 2002b)

Activity 29 helps you to locate this important guidance and to consider its implications for social work with children and young people who offend.

Allow about 1 hour

Website

## Activity 29   National Standards for Youth Justice Services

Following the link from this activity on the course website, read the *National Standards for Youth Justice Services*. You will find it useful to bookmark the link to this document for future use. From this document, and the material that you have read so far in this block, make brief notes in answer to the following questions:

1   What do these standards cover?

2   What are 'youth justice services'?

3   What is a youth justice team?

4   What is the priority for youth justice teams?

5   What tensions do you think the standards might present for effective and ethical social work practice within children's services?

## Comment

At the current time these standards are much less comprehensive than those issued for criminal justice social work. Rather than providing detailed guidance for practice they indicate key processes that must be undertaken within given timeframes and the services that should be made available to tackle youth offending. It is anticipated that further guidance will follow, on for example the content of social work action plans and supervision, as youth justice policy develops.

This document refers throughout to a youth justice system or process that is not easy to identify in the current legal arrangements in Scotland. We have seen that in fact there are parallel 'processes' in operation. Therefore, while the aim of the reform programme and these standards is to streamline the coordination of these 'services' to achieve better outcomes for young people who offend and their communities, the translation of these requirements into action is far from straightforward. The standards apply to all 'partners' in youth justice services (the police, local authorities, Scottish Children's Reporter Administration, hearings, procurator fiscals and the voluntary sector). Most of the individual standards, however, relate solely to the children's hearings system, tightening up practice requirements for young people referred to the reporter on offence grounds (standardised assessment tools and the provision of social work action plans) and ensuring a range of offence-related interventions for young people under supervision and that these requirements are implemented.

Youth justice teams are central to the achievement of these objectives. Usually sited within children's services they are responsible for effective liaison with partner agencies, the assessment of young people, the monitoring and evaluation of offence-related programmes and the publication of annual performance information to their local communities. Inter-agency strategy groups are responsible for the planning and coordination of youth justice services and feed into the preparation of local authorities' children's services plans.

You may have noted that the National Standards for Youth Justice Services add a new layer of accountability and policy guidance to children's services, that are specific to offence-related practice and addressing offending behaviour. This is something of a departure for the integrated children's hearing system that has traditionally been focused on the welfare needs of children and young people, regardless of their reasons for referral. It fits within the current legal framework, which you should recall allows hearings to make decisions that are not in the best interests of the child in order to protect others (s. 16(5) Children (Scotland) Act), but has the potential to heighten tensions between welfare and justice that are inherent in the social work role. For example, meeting the target for the reduction of persistent offenders is stated to be the priority of every youth justice team 'although, of course, their work will also include implementing early intervention measures that prevent offending and diverting young people from becoming persistent offenders' (Scottish Executive, 2002b, p. 3). This direction has implications for the targeting of resources within wider children's services and does little to resolve the often conflicting demands in this area.

The social work practice setting is therefore undergoing a process of change as a result of policy developments that arguably direct the service away from an integrated welfare focus and foster an emerging specialist youth justice social work role. It is currently unclear how this will impact on the Kilbrandon response to children who offend, although it is likely to pose some dilemmas in choices about service provision. The introduction of national standards, however, could also be said to enhance Scotland's compliance with UNCRC provisions, by working towards the prompt resolution of children's cases, and making the social work contribution to the children's hearings process more accountable.

Given the pace of change in this area it is important that you keep up to date with policy and legislative developments. Activity 30 enables you to find information on youth justice in Scotland.

Allow about 40 minutes

Website

## Activity 30   Keeping up to date with youth justice services

Follow the link from this activity on the course website to the Scottish Executive's youth justice site. Click on the 'News' section of the toolbar at the top of the page, where you will find links to the most recent policy documents and initiatives. Select the most recent document that relates to reform and/or the National Standards and make a brief note of its contents.

### Comment

This website is excellent for obtaining up-to-date information on youth justice in Scotland. The 'Library' section also provides a searchable database of relevant publications, for example it contains information on the Children's Hearings Review, the Youth Justice Improvement Group, updates on the ten-point action plan and the implementation of national standards. You can also browse the Scottish Executive's Youth Justice site according to key themes and will find it provides access to a wide range of material, including research findings and practice guidance.

You should remember, however, that there are other available resources, including non-governmental sites, journals and databases where you can find research and often more critical comment on recent developments. You will find information about these under the library resources section of the course website and links to criminal justice organisations in the course Directory. All relevant information on legislative developments, for example in relation to the Children's Hearings Review, will be posted in the news section of the course website and included in future update supplements.

You should now have a better understanding of the legal processes that underpin youth justice in Scotland and the social work role. The next sections will take a closer look at separate stages in this process (contact with the police, the children's hearings system and the criminal justice system) and the various disposals that are available for children and young people.

## 3.5 Police intervention

We have seen that the police are often the first point of contact between children and the formal legal process and that interactions between the police and young people can help to shape social perceptions of youth crime and antisocial behaviour. The police are important gatekeepers of the criminal justice and children's hearings system and their decisions, on whether to report and who to report an alleged young offender to, are crucial.

In their contact with the police, children are entitled to the same rights and protections that are available to adults within the criminal justice system (see Activity 12). There are, however, additional provisions that apply that take into account the vulnerability of young people in the police station.

When a person is detained or arrested who appears to be a child under the age of 16 the police are obliged to inform their parents that they are in police custody and where they are being held. Parents for this purpose include guardians or any person who has custody of a child. Where the police have reasonable cause to believe that the child has been involved in an offence they may allow the parent to have access to them; in all other cases they must allow parental access (s. 15(4) Criminal Procedure (Scotland) Act 1995). This is subject to restrictions where it is essential for the furtherance of an investigation (for example if there is a suspicion that the parent may be involved in the crime) or the well-being of the child.

Parents in Scotland do not have to be present when a child is interviewed by the police, but where a child is considered to be vulnerable (because, for example, they may not understand what is being put to them) guidance obliges the police to conduct an interview in the presence of an 'appropriate adult'. This will usually be a parent or guardian but may involve a social work presence where, for example, the child is looked after by a local authority. While there is no legal requirement on the police to have an appropriate adult present in all cases involving children and young people, the Scottish courts take a very strict view on fairness to the accused. If there is a suggestion that a young person has been inappropriately interviewed, the evidence is likely to be inadmissible. The role of an appropriate adult is considered further in Section 4 of this block. They do not act as a legal representative or advocate for the child but are present to facilitate communication.

As indicated in Figure 10, after charge the police have some discretion (subject to the Lord Advocate's guidance) over whether to refer the case to the children's reporter, the procurator fiscal, or both. In addition they have the power to decide (either in consultation or alone) to dispose of the case themselves, either informally or by way of a police warning. Box 25 explains the meaning of a police warning as an example of early diversion from the legal process.

### Box 25 Police restorative warnings

'A process, facilitated by trained personnel that involves the warning of an offender whilst addressing the impact on the victim and the community. The victim will have the opportunity to be informed of the outcome.'

A restorative warning:

- is an early formal recorded intervention to reduce the likelihood of re-offending amongst youth offenders, frequently first and sometimes subsequent youth offenders;
- can (and should) be done quickly;
- must be carried out by officers trained in restorative warning methods;
- impresses upon the young person the impact of the offence on the victim or the community and on his/her parents, encouraging him/her to take responsibility for his/her actions and to understand the implications of future offending;
- is focused on changing the behaviour and attitude of the young person rather than on humiliating him/her; and
- takes account of victim issues in that the victim is made aware that the warning is taking place, has the opportunity to make known the impact of the offence, and if he/she wants, is informed of the outcome from the warning.

(Scottish Executive 2004i, para. 3)

A police warning may take the form of a restorative conference in the presence of the victim and with possible involvement with social workers, teachers and friends. This will depend on the needs of the victim.

From April 2006 all police warnings given to young people under the age of 16 are expected to be restorative. Police have wide discretion over whether to choose this option but should seek the advice of the children's reporter to establish whether there are additional welfare grounds that would warrant referral to the children's hearings system.

The usual criteria for issuing a warning are:

- the case involves a minor offence
- there has been no previous offending or referral to the reporter
- there are no welfare concerns
- the young person admits the offence
- the parent accepts the admission, and
- both the young person and the parent consent to a warning.

Police may use their discretion to give a warning for more serious offences and/or, where there is a prior record of offending, if they believe the accused is susceptible to a restorative approach.

Restorative warnings were introduced with Scottish Executive funding with an aim to prevent the escalation of minor offending and avoid further contact with legal processes. They have the additional benefit of freeing up resources in the children's hearings system. It is too early to evaluate the impact of these disposals on reducing reoffending in Scotland but research studies into the pilot programmes have shown high levels of satisfaction with warnings and restorative conferences amongst young people, victims and professionals. Evidence from existing restorative justice evaluations suggests that this approach in isolation performs no better than other forms of diversion in reducing reoffending, but when integrated with other services addressing the needs of young people it is more likely to be effective (Dutton and Whyte, 2006).

Activity 31 asks you to consider how the youth justice system might respond to a young person who is on the verge of drifting into offending behaviour.

Allow about 30 minutes

## Activity 31   James's story

Read the case below and using the youth justice processes flow diagram in Figure 10 and your understanding of the available legal options make notes in answer to the questions that follow.

> James is 14. He lives with his mother and younger sister in the city centre. His mother has a full-time job and the family are relatively well provided for. James attends the local secondary school. Over the last few months his teachers have noticed a decline in his interest and participation. During the evenings James spends his time with a group of friends. They sometimes play football but mostly hang about the streets. They have recently begun drinking cider, which they obtain from one of the local shops. James and his friends have increasingly been coming to the attention of the police, who have moved them on various occasions. They also had to take James home on one occasion because he was intoxicated. Last night James and his friends were caught smashing windows of a vacant shop

1   What options do the police have in dealing with James?

2   What do you think should happen to him now?

## Comment

In James's case relatively minor acts of youthful antisocial behaviour have escalated into the commission of an offence. This is clearly concerning and it is possible that if left unchecked he will increasingly become involved in offending behaviour. James is not yet, however, a persistent offender and various steps could be taken now to try to prevent him progressing along these lines.

The police have already had some informal involvement with James and their involvement alone has not been enough to curb his actions. As there is now sufficient evidence to result in a charge the police are likely to take formal action. James apparently meets the criteria for a police restorative warning, although before this option is taken the police would have to seek the advice of the children's reporter on whether further investigation was necessary into James's welfare needs. James and his parents would also have to agree to this process. There is, however, a problem here as the shop was vacant, and while the legal owner would be an identifiable victim, the police may consider that their account of the impact of the offence would be unlikely to encourage James to face up to the consequences of his offence and take responsibility for his behaviour.

Alternatively, the police could decide to formally notify the reporter, who has a number of further options: taking no further action, arranging a voluntary referral to social services or remitting the case to the children's hearing on offence grounds.

At a children's hearing James would be required to account for his behaviour. His mother would also be present. The hearing could decide to place James on a supervision order. However, a more constructive way of dealing with his case may be to defer the outcome for a period of time and refer him to a local youth project or community group. There are various projects run jointly by community education and the social work departments which aim to intervene with young people like James. The remit of these projects is wide, looking at social skill development, structured use of time, creating a sense of belonging and educating young people about their rights and responsibilities. It is likely that a project like this would be of more use to James than a more punitive offence-weighted programme and might divert him from further and more serious involvement in offending behaviour.

## 3.6 Referral to the children's hearings system

The majority of referrals to the children's reporter on offence grounds come from the police, although it is important to recognise that other agencies, including for example local authority antisocial behaviour coordinators, may submit a report. The fact that a case is brought to the attention of the reporter on these grounds, however, does not mean that it will be taken forward on that basis. The reporter has an important role as gatekeeper of the children's hearings system and under the provisions of the Children (Scotland) Act 1995 can only refer to a panel hearing a child whom they consider meets one of the grounds for referral and may be in need of compulsory supervision. A decision-making framework guides this process and attempts to balance the principles of minimum intervention with the welfare needs of the child (SCRA, 2005). The gravity alone of the offence referred is not, therefore, the sole determinant of the reporter's decision. Offending behaviour may be indicative of specific welfare needs but investigation by the reporter could establish the need for referral to the panel on other grounds, or lead to the conclusion that no compulsory intervention is necessary. In this way the reporter has a function in diverting young offenders from further involvement in the legal process and preventing the potential for 'welfare creep' in the reach of youth justice interventions.

While offence referrals make up a small proportion of the overall number of cases brought to the attention of the children's reporter, concerns have been raised in recent years about an increase in these types of referrals and the ability of the children's hearings system to cope. We have seen that the rise in so-called 'persistent' offenders has become a focus of government youth justice policy (despite making up only around 3 per cent of the children referred to the reporter in 2005/6) and that the children's hearing system is now at the centre of youth justice reforms. Information on the social work role in the children's hearings system was covered in Block 2. This section will highlight key aspects of the changes to the legal framework in relation to youth justice and consider their implications for social work practice.

### Victims

One of the aims of the National Standards for Youth Justice Services (see Box 24) was to improve the information provided to victims of youth crime whose cases are referred to the children's hearings system. There was a concern that because this diverts offenders from the criminal justice process the interests of the victim were being overlooked and, in the absence of a prosecution, justice was not seen to be done. National standards now require that every victim should receive information about the process for dealing with the young person who has committed an offence against them and the outcome of that process. Under the National Standards for Victims of Crime (see Activity 9), this is now the responsibility of the children's reporter. Where appropriate, victims may also have the opportunity to engage with mediation or reparation schemes provided by social work services.

## Delays

The National Standards for Youth Justice Services also aim to reduce the time taken from the initial report on an offender to the children's reporter, to the implementation of a hearing decision (which now should take place within 80 days). Time limits have been set on the work of all relevant agencies, including the police, the reporter and social work. The avoidance of delay is a rights-based principle that is reflected in both the UNCRC and the Children (Scotland) Act 1995, and the National Standards significantly reinforce this aim.

Implementation of these standards, however, raises tensions for practitioners, who must meet a range of obligations within resource constraints. Following the conclusion of a fast-track pilot scheme for persistent offenders (which ended in 2005 and was not shown to have a significant effect on reoffending rates compared to other local authorities) the Scottish Executive has provided funding to all 32 local authorities to help them to meet the National Standards commitment of a fast-track hearing in all offence-based cases. There is a danger, however, that the legal framework's strengthened offence orientation could lead to a two-tier hearings system, with scarce resources being targeted at the immediate demands of dealing with offending children, rather than realising the goals of the Kilbrandon approach. Social workers are well placed to advocate the importance of supporting all service users and their families, without unduly prioritising offence-based interventions. In accordance with the promotion of children's rights, the value of ensuring effective and timely management of all cases involving children should inform their practice across children's services, not just in the area of youth justice where specific guidance applies.

## Enhanced service provision

The National Standards acknowledge that 'no single programme or intervention has all the answers to reducing offending' but they have put in place structures to ensure that local differences in service provision do not prevent access to appropriate and effective offence-based interventions. These are expected to include the following community programmes:

- intensive community-based support and supervision
- restorative justice approaches
- family/parent support
- cognitive skills
- anger management
- alcohol, drugs and mental health programmes
- diversionary projects.

Emphasis has been placed on improving assessment of a young person's offending behaviour and the reasons for that behaviour, within an integrated assessment framework. Youth justice teams are required to use the Asset or YLS-CMI assessment tools for all referrals on offence grounds and to produce an action plan based on this assessment, to be presented to the children's hearing. Box 26 outlines the requirements of an action plan as currently described in the National Standards.

---

**Box 26 Offence-based action plans**

An action plan must be submitted within twenty working days of the Reporter's request.

The action plan will state the options for the programme/ interventions to be followed; who will deliver them; the case management arrangements and the intensity of contact and supervision required.

Every action plan will be reviewed within two months of the initial hearing by the young person's case manager. The action plan should be updated and reviewed within three months of the first review and at intervals agreed between the case manager, young person and others as appropriate, thereafter endorsed by the reporter and further hearing, when necessary.

The programmes recommended in the action plan must be available.

(Adapted from Scottish Executive, 2002b)

---

Asset and the YLS-CMI are structured assessment tools designed specifically for use with young people. They allow for the assessment of both risk of reoffending and offence-related needs and are comparable to those used in criminal justice social work (as described in Section 2.6 under 'Risk assessment'). Asset was developed by the Youth Justice Board in England and Wales, whereas the YLS-CMI was developed in Canada and has been adopted by a number of local authorities in Scotland. In Section 2 you were introduced to some of the limitations of these structured methods of assessment. Activity 32 helps you to see the potential for such assessment tools to aid professional judgement and values-based practice in youth justice teams.

---

Allow about 40 minutes

## Activity 32   Assessing the risk of offending behaviour

Website

Following the link from this activity on the course website, read the 'Introduction' to Asset, the 'What do you think? Guidance' and Examples 1 and 2 (Robin's case) in the 'case material' published by the Youth Justice Board. It is important to remember that the legal guidance and sentencing orders described in these documents do not apply in Scotland and you are therefore asked to focus on the method of assessment as an aid to effective practice. When reading Robin's case (Examples 1 and 2 in the case materials) consider the following scenario:

---

Robin is a 15-year-old boy who is looked after by the local authority after having been placed under a supervision requirement by a children's hearing. He was referred to the hearing on offence grounds for offences of violence committed against other pupils at school. He describes himself as white, British.

After reading these extracts, make notes in answer to the following questions:

1   What factors are part of the core profile assessment in Asset?

2   Do any of these also relate to general (non-offence-based) welfare concerns?

3   Why is the 'What do you think?' section part of this assessment?

4   How can this contribute to rights-based practice?

## Comment

This activity should have reinforced your understanding of the close relationship between criminogenic risk factors and the welfare needs of young offenders. In Robin's case there are clearly issues in relation to his family and personal relationships that are in need of support, in addition to problems more directly associated with his offence (e.g. cognitive behavioural issues requiring anger management).

It also demonstrates that the assessment process works best in partnership with the young person, whose rights are better respected given the opportunity to participate in their assessment and the plans for future intervention. Local authorities are required to take into account the child's views when making any decision in relation to a child that they propose to look after (s. 17(3) Children (Scotland) Act 1995) and this can be built into a structured assessment. Such participation is also the basis for desistence-based approaches that were introduced in Section 1.4 of this block as empowering strategies for addressing reoffending.

Risk assessment is also a key means of ensuring accountability in social work practice:

> In recognition of the inherent unpredictability of future behaviour, it is generally accepted that 'defensibility' rather than 'certainty' is the goal of risk assessment practice. A 'defensible' risk assessment is one which is judged to be as accurate as possible and which would stand up to scrutiny if the handling of the case were to be investigated.
>
> (Robinson (2003) quoted in McNeill and Batchelor, 2004, p. 38)

A difficulty in youth justice practice in Scotland, however, is the relationship between offence-related assessment and the social worker's obligations to assess a child's needs and to protect and promote the rights of children (McNeill and Batchelor, 2004, p. 41). How these tools will fit within the Integrated Assessment Framework and guide decisions about how and when to intervene with children and young people with multiple and complex needs will continue to raise questions for practice. For example, in Robin's case above, where there is evidence that his carer (his mother) is involved in heavy alcohol abuse, how do you balance the risks posed to Robin and his sister with the risks posed by Robin in considering a suitable plan of action?

In the youth justice context the responsibility of parents for their children's behaviour has become an increasing policy focus. The children's hearings system can place compulsory conditions only on the child who is subject to a supervision order, not on his or her parents. The local authority and/or the children's reporter do, however, have an alternative course of legal action to force the involvement of parents in this process, as Box 27 outlines.

---

**Box 27 Parenting orders**

The Antisocial Behaviour etc. (Scotland) Act 2004 sections 103 to 117 introduced parenting orders by which the sheriff court can order a parent to comply with any requirements, including their attendance at counselling or guidance sessions.

The local authority or the reporter may apply for this order and they must consult with each other before doing so. The children's hearing panel also has the power to direct the reporter to apply.

The local authority can only apply on grounds related to the child's criminal conduct or antisocial behaviour. The reporter can in addition apply for an order where it is desirable in the interests of improving the welfare of the child. The local authority and the reporter must consult each other before applying for an order.

A parenting order is a civil order but breach of the order is an offence that is punishable on summary conviction with a fine not exceeding level 3 on the standard scale.

---

At the time of writing no parenting orders have been made in Scotland. This is arguably because in a welfare-oriented system the fostering of more inclusive partnership working is preferred to formal action that can stigmatise and potentially punish 'failing' parents. The relationship between parent and child, however, is often crucial in responding to offending behaviour, as the example in Box 28 shows.

---

**Box 28 Aberlour National Parenting Project**

In 2002 the Scottish Executive provided four years of funding from their Youth Crime Prevention Fund for the charity Aberlour Childcare Trust to develop and promote parenting programmes in Scotland.

One example is the Aberdeen Youth Justice Parenting Teenagers Support Group, a pilot programme jointly run by Aberlour and the Aberdeen Youth Justice Fieldwork Team. This was targeted by assessment at parents of teenagers, aged 14–16 years, whose children are involved in offending behaviour (either convicted of offences or referred to the reporter or social work on offence grounds). The objectives of the group were:

To *develop parenting skills and knowledge*.

To *improve parents' confidence*, their *sense of coping and abilities* to address their children's behaviour.

To try to actively *involve fathers*, male partners and those involved in a substantive caring role in any intervention.

To *improve parent/child interactions* and communications.

> To *increase positive supervision and monitoring* of the children and young people by the parents.
>
> To *aid consistent, non-physical discipline.*
>
> To involve *parents* in collecting their *views* on their needs, service delivery and the future planning of parent related work.
>
> (Rioch and Manson, 2006)
>
> Evaluation of the project showed that parenting programmes can be effective in terms of increasing the parents' positive perceptions of their child, increasing parental self confidence and sense of coping, and improving children's emotional and prosocial behaviour. Ensuring parental engagement in the project proved to be difficult in some cases, particularly where parents' ongoing mental health issues, incidents of domestic abuse, and chaotic lifestyles made it difficult to progress. The development of a supportive and non-judgemental environment was of prime importance to the success of these projects.

### Secure accommodation and the restriction of movement

Although youth justice social workers clearly have professional discretion in the assessment of children and young people and the recommendations in their action plans, once a supervision requirement is made the National Standards require them to implement every supervision requirement made by a hearing. This is subject to only one exception – the discretion of the chief social work officer in relation to secure authorisation.

The authorisation of secure accommodation under section 70(10) of the Children (Scotland) Act 1995 can be made only where the hearing is satisfied that the following conditions are met:

- The young person has previously absconded, is likely to abscond unless kept in secure accommodation, and if they abscond his or her physical, mental or moral welfare is in danger; or
- The young person is likely to injure him or herself or some other person unless kept in secure accommodation.

The general principles of the Children (Scotland) Act apply, namely that secure placements should be only for so long as it is in the best interests of the child. Social workers have an important role to play in the decision to use secure care. Recent research has suggested that their experience and confidence in safely managing risk through effective assessment, case management and the provision of intensive community-based services could enable some young people to be supported outside of a secure setting (Walker et al., 2006).

Commentators have expressed some concern over the expansion of secure accommodation as part of the youth crime strategy, arguing that this is a welfare rather than a 'justice' oriented disposal (Smith and Milligan, 2004). The introduction of additional places was based on the need for separate provision for girls and young women, and the need to avoid under-16s being placed in young offender institutions (both rights-based concerns). They were framed by the Scottish Executive, however, within the wider debate about youth crime and persistent offending.

National standards aim to reduce the number of young people re-referred to secure accommodation on offence grounds and introduce new requirements for case management, throughcare, aftercare and the introduction of accredited 'what works' programmes in these settings. Critics have suggested that increased specialism in units will lead to longer periods of confinement in secure accommodation, less flexibility in the secure estate and may draw funding away from other areas of residential childcare where preventative programmes could have a greater effect (Smith and Milligan, 2004).

Social workers and secure care managers need to balance these conflicting demands within the current policy context and avoid defensive practice by improving service provision. They should also be aware that there are potential human rights issues in this area. The human rights implications of the detention of children in secure care were raised in the case of *S v. Miller* (2001) SC 977 where it was argued that secure accommodation breached the child's right to liberty under Article 5 of the European Convention on Human Rights (ECHR). The Court of Session ruled that detention of a minor was lawful where it was for the purpose of educational supervision and maintained that secure care amounted to educational supervision on behalf of the local authority 'parent' as it was for the benefit and protection of the child concerned. This is a rather flexible interpretation of the ECHR provisions, and further legal challenge could be possible (for example if a child's stay in secure accommodation was prolonged for the purpose of completing an offence-related programme).

Where a child or young person is assessed as being of high risk to themselves or others and meets the criteria for secure accommodation, the Antisocial Behaviour etc. (Scotland) Act 2004 introduced an alternative to secure care that is outlined in Box 29.

---

**Box 29  Restriction of movement: Intensive Supervision and Monitoring Services (ISMS)**

The Antisocial Behaviour etc. (Scotland) Act 2004 amended section 70 of the Children (Scotland) Act 1995 to allow for the children's hearing to impose a 'movement restriction condition' where the criteria for secure accommodation is met. The movement restriction condition, or 'tagging' as it is more commonly known, allows the child or young person to stay in an open setting while proscribing their movement at certain times and to certain places.

The Scottish Executive is currently piloting Intensive Supervision and Monitoring Services (ISMS). When a person is assessed as needing a movement restriction this is combined with the provision of intensive community-based services to address the young person's complex needs and provide support. They will be allocated a case manager who is responsible for monitoring their performance on their programme of intervention and compliance with electronic monitoring. Where a person cannot be located the police will be notified that they are a missing person. ISMS requirements are reviewed by the children's hearing after three months.

The introduction of 'tagging' to the children's hearings system has proved controversial as it is normally associated with the criminal justice sphere. Initial reports on the pilot programmes suggest that the take-up of ISMS has been low, with local authorities preferring to fund intensive support services which address offending behaviour, rather than the electronic monitoring element, which is often breached (Adams, 2006).

### Persistent offenders

These legislative developments in relation to high-end service provision have been motivated by a concern to tackle the problem of persistent offenders that has increasingly preoccupied policy makers and practitioners alike since the 1990s. Activity 33 helps you to think about some of the issues this problem raises for those working with young people who offend.

Allow about 30 minutes

Website

### Activity 33   Persistent offenders

It is important to understand the nature of this problem and the difficulties that it raises for social workers, the courts and the hearings system. Following the link from this activity on the course website, read the extract by Whyte (1998) and make notes on the following questions.

1   What is meant by the term 'persistent offenders'?

2   What are the common characteristics shared by young persistent offenders?

3   Why do they present problems for the hearings system?

### Comment

As you have read, it is now well established that, at any one time, a small proportion of young offenders are responsible for a disproportionate amount of criminal activity. This awareness has given rise to renewed attempts to define 'persistence' and to identify new models of intervention for those who commit either serious or numerous offences. There is, however, evidence that punishing young people by locking them up does not help to tackle the problem of persistent offending and makes little difference to overall crime levels. Whyte cautions against the current trend of designing policy and practice around persistent offenders and argues that any definition will inevitably be arbitrary and lead to inequity if responses are based solely on offence grounds.

Whyte suggests that the children's hearings system has hitherto been ineffective in dealing with the needs and deeds of these high risk groups. It is not that their characteristics are markedly different from young people whose offending is infrequent, but their personal and social problems are often more entrenched and complex. In some cases this can be seen as a failing of the system itself, where for example a child has already been in residential care and deteriorates following discharge. It is also clear that persistent offenders are more likely to be referred to the procurator fiscal and few of these cases are referred back to the hearings system for a response.

Research into social work practice suggests that social workers who encounter young people involved in persistent offending often adopt a pessimistic approach centred on containment (care and protection) rather than behavioural change:

> Put simply, when the chaos in the young people's lives met pressure of work and caseloads for the social workers concerned, this generated containment as a practice response. Put bluntly, the case-files read as if they thought that this was the best that they could do and the most that they could expect.
>
> (McNeill and Batchelor, 2004, p. 36)

Against this context the recent focus on improving access to intensive support services and evaluating programmes for their impact on effecting change better promotes the values of the social work profession. Social workers in both the statutory and voluntary sectors can make a positive contribution to the development of interventions that address persistent offending. For example, programmes that allow young people to address their behaviour and develop their social skills and that introduce them to aggression reduction techniques can all help. Social workers can also engage in inter-professional collaborations with other agencies, such as schools and the police, to develop comprehensive strategies and projects for preventing crime and offending. Because of the difficulties in defining persistence it is often hard to identify those most in need of intervention before they have been drawn within the criminal justice process. Early intervention programmes supporting children and families in their communities and addressing the marginalisation and social exclusion experienced by some young people may be more effective. Crime is complex and multifaceted and so demands solutions that encompass a range of dimensions.

Activity 34 provides an example of one of Scotland's established programmes for persistent young offenders.

---

Allow about 30 minutes | **Activity 34   Understanding intensive support services**

Website

Following the link from this activity on the course website, read the Scottish Executive research findings 'Freagarrach: an Evaluation of a Project for Persistent Juvenile Offenders' and make notes in answer to the following questions:

1   Who were the target group for the Freagarrach project?

2   What does the programme involve?

3   What is the evidence of its effectiveness?

### Comment

Freagarrach accepts social work referrals of young people aged 12–16 years who have been involved in at least five episodes of offending in the previous twelve months, where offending is the main reason for agency involvement. This has recently been extended up to the age of 18 years as the project also accepts referrals from criminal justice social work.

Freagarrach is an intensive supervision service that takes a holistic, welfare-based approach to address offending behaviour, for example by promoting victim awareness and reparation, cognitive behavioural work, responding to any employment or educational problems, addressing family issues and promoting the constructive use of leisure time. This involves individual discussion, group work and recreational activities. There is evidence that the project leads to a reduction in reoffending, changing the rate and seriousness of offending behaviour and contributing to a lower use of custody. There are also indications that attendance has helped to improve some young people's family relationships and removed or delayed their entry to the care system (Buist, 2005).

The quality of available community programmes can therefore divert young people from secure care and from being drawn further into the criminal justice process. At the same time as developing the effectiveness of these programmes, however, the Scottish Executive has been piloting a new criminal justice response to persistent offenders aged 16–17 (defined for this purpose as a person with three or more referrals to the procurator fiscal in a three month period). These youth court pilots will be discussed in Section 3.7 below, but before considering the position of children and young people in the criminal justice process you need to understand the limitations of the children's hearings system in relation to this age group.

### 16–17 year olds

Although the majority of children under 16 who commit offences are dealt with by the children's hearing system, this is not the case with 16 and 17 year olds. If a young person aged 16 or 17 is subject to a supervision requirement, he or she is defined as a child for the purposes of the Children (Scotland) Act 1995 and so could be referred to a hearing rather than a criminal court if an offence is committed. In practice, however, procurators fiscal normally prosecute 16 and 17 year olds who are on supervision unless there are special circumstances. It is unclear whether procurators fiscal have sufficient information on the social background of young people to allow them to decide whether a young person should be dealt with by the children's hearing system or an adult criminal court. Section 27(1)(ab) of the Social Work (Scotland) Act 1968 empowers the procurator fiscal to ask the local authority to provide a social background report on a 16 or 17 year old and the local authority must comply with this request. Young people who are not on supervision must be prosecuted in a criminal court. (You will find it helpful to refer back to the youth justice processes diagram in Figure 10 at this stage.)

In addition, the legal framework provides further opportunities for a criminal case to be referred back to the children's hearing system for advice and/or disposal. These are summarised in Box 30.

> **Box 30 Court referral to the children's hearings system**
>
> Under section 49 of the Criminal Procedure (Scotland) Act 1995 criminal courts have the power, and sometimes a duty, to refer children and young people to the children's hearing for advice and/or disposal of a criminal case in the following circumstances.
>
> • If a child under 16 and not subject to a supervision requirement pleads guilty or is found guilty, the court may refer the child to the principal reporter to arrange for a hearing to dispose of the case or to give advice to the court on sentencing. Upon

receipt of the advice, the court may remit the case back to the hearing for disposal or may dispose of the case itself.

- If a child under 18 and already subject to a supervision requirement pleads guilty or is found guilty, the sheriff court must and the High Court may refer the child to the principal reporter to arrange a hearing for advice on sentencing. Upon receipt of that advice, the court may remit the case back to the hearing for disposal or dispose of the case itself.

- If a child over 16 but not yet 17 years and 6 months who is not subject to a supervision requirement pleads guilty or is found guilty, a summary court may refer the case to the principal reporter to arrange a hearing for advice on sentencing. Upon receipt of this advice, the court may remit the case back to the hearing for disposal or may dispose of the case itself. This is the only situation where a hearing may impose a supervision requirement on a child over 16 who is not already subject to supervision.

These interactions between the criminal justice process and the children's hearings system are quite complex and it is important that social workers understand the possibilities that exist within the legal framework to divert young offenders from the criminal justice process. Social workers, for example, could recommend diversion to the children's hearing system for disposal in a social enquiry report (SER) for the criminal court.

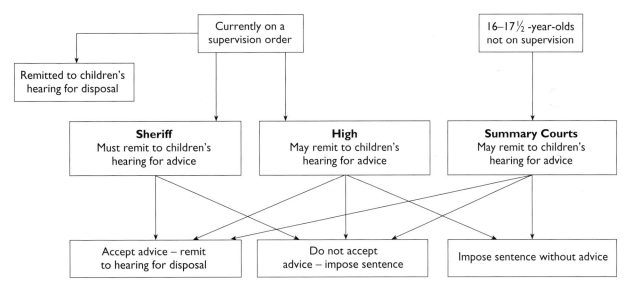

Figure 12   Options for 16 and 17 year olds charged with an offence

The social work role here is significant because research suggests that when young people near their 16th birthday and they have a history of offending behaviour, their supervision orders are not likely to be renewed. Kennedy and McIvor (1992) examined SERs on 182 young people aged between 15 and 17 requested from one regional social work department over a six-month period. They found that 53 per cent of the sample had made previous appearances before the children's hearing and all but one had been on supervision in the past. Most had been discharged from the system at the age of 16 with their offending unresolved. Things improved slightly in 2005/6: of the 17,624 referrals to reporters on offence grounds, over 1,000 were for 16 year olds and 184 cases were referred to the reporter by the sheriff court. This still represents a minority of cases involving the 16–17 age group.

Moore and Whyte observe:

> empirical data ... gives some weight to the view that the most persistent offenders are discharged prematurely from the system only to face the full force of the adult system shortly afterwards. Available statistical data gives some support to the view, not so much that the hearing system is unable to deal with the young person in this age group who offends, but that it simply does not do so. Intentionally or otherwise, it normally passes them readily to the adult system. The adult system, in turn, does not seem to view the hearing system as an obvious route for dealing with those under 18 years appearing before it.
>
> (Moore and Whyte, 1998, p. 168)

In 1997 the Crime and Punishment (Scotland) Act 1997 amended section 27 (1) of the Social Work (Scotland) Act 1968 to extend 100 per cent central government funding to providing additional services that support diversion from prosecution. Such services include the production of reports by social work departments where 16 and 17 year olds have committed offences that are dealt with by the children's hearing system. This change was introduced in an attempt to ensure that such young people were involved with the adult criminal justice system only if this was appropriate and not because of inadequate financial resourcing. Under these amended provisions the supervision of 16 and 17 year olds by social workers, within the terms of section 70 of the Children (Scotland) Act 1995, could be funded entirely by central government. This is in keeping with the broad principles of the children's hearings system, which place emphasis on diverting young people away from the criminal justice process. It is also intended to reduce the costs of the system. As a result a number of diversion schemes that target this age group have been developed. The extension of the Freagarrach project to include 16–18 year olds in 1999 is one example.

It is important to remember that the imposition of a compulsory supervision requirement is not the only route to social work support. The provisions of the Children (Scotland) Act 1995 could also be used to offer services to young people under 18. You will remember from Block 2 that a child 'in need' in terms of section 22 includes young people up to 18 years of age, and that the local authority has a duty to safeguard and promote the welfare of such children. Also, the local authority has a duty to draw up children's services plans (s. 19) for children in its area, and this would include services for children who offend. There is scope for coordination and collaboration between social workers engaged in childcare and those involved in criminal justice to share their knowledge and skills in planning and developing services for young people who offend.

In 2000 a key recommendation of the Youth Crime Review was that there should be substantial investment in specialist provision to allow the children's hearings to retain young people beyond the age of 15 years who were involved in persistent offending (Scottish Executive, 2000). Bridging pilots were suggested as a means of ensuring more flexible transition between the hearings system and criminal justice process and that the welfare needs of this group were met. Instead the idea of a youth court operating outwith the children's hearings system is currently being piloted for persistent offenders.

## 3.7 Children and young people in the criminal justice process

In 2004/5, 27,545 young people under the age of 21 had a charge proved against them in a criminal court (Scottish Executive, 2006a). Most were over the age of 14. Care for the welfare of children and young people within the criminal justice context is part of the responsibility of criminal justice social work. Subject to the special arrangements outlined below, children and young people follow the same process as that outlined in Section 2 for adults.

### Children at court

There are certain protective measures in place to ensure that the welfare of children (under 16 or over 16 and subject to supervision) is considered in the court system. For example:

- When a child is charged or arrested, the police officer is required to notify a parent or guardian, if he or she can be found, and to 'warn them of their duty to attend the court' (s. 42(2)(3) Criminal Procedure (Scotland) Act 1995).
- If a child is to be prosecuted on either summary or solemn procedure, the chief constable has to inform the local authority of the charge, and of the date and time of the court appearance (s. 42(7) of the same Act).
- The local authority is then obliged to investigate and submit a report about the child and his or her circumstances and a school report will be included in this (s. 42(8) of the Act).
- The criminal court is required to have regard to the welfare of the child (s. 50(6) of the Act). Note that this is not the same as the welfare principle in the Children (Scotland) Act 1995, where the welfare of the child is paramount.
- Child witnesses under the age of 16 are classed as vulnerable under the Vulnerable Witnesses (Scotland) Act 2004 and are entitled to special measures when giving evidence in court (see Block 1, Section 2.4 and the Law Resource summary for details).

When a child is arrested, he or she will usually be freed on an undertaking to appear at court. This undertaking can be given by the child, or the parent or guardian. In certain circumstances a child may not be set free, but will be kept in a place of safety. The place of safety should be somewhere provided by the local authority, not a police station. It could be a children's home or, less commonly, a placement with foster carers. However, the local authority can refuse to accommodate a child if he or she is designated as being unruly. Moore and Whyte report that:

> Anecdotal evidence suggests that ... there is a growing problem of children being detained in remand centres on unruly certificates that needs to be addressed by improved liaison ... between social work and the police.
>
> (Moore and Whyte, 1998, p. 123)

The development of remand fostering schemes aim to avoid the inappropriate use of detention. These are explained in Box 31.

> ### Box 31 Remand fostering
>
> NCH Scotland provide a remand fostering service in North Lanarkshire to support the Hamilton Youth Court pilot. Instead of remand into custody or secure accommodation this service places young people aged 16–17 with specially trained foster carers who are able to cope with young people who may have a history of aggression or drug use. The carers are provided with intensive support and supervision and can assist the young people to address their offending behaviour and other needs.

If a child is found guilty the court will have an opportunity to read the social background reports prepared by the social worker in terms of section 42(8) of the Criminal Procedure (Scotland) Act 1995. The court may also have referred the case to a children's hearing for advice and/ or disposal.

The court has a wide range of sentencing powers when dealing with children and young people who have been found guilty of offences. These include many of those available to adult offenders, except that the court cannot make a community service order or a probation order that includes a requirement for unpaid work where the offender is under the age of 16 (see Table 3 on sentencing disposals). Special provisions also apply to the detention of young offenders, who cannot be sentenced to imprisonment.

These adaptations to the adult criminal justice process arguably do not fully comply with the UNCRC, which you will remember requires the procedure to be 'consistent with the promotion of the child's sense of dignity and worth' and to take into account the child's age. There is no separate court room or noticeably different procedure for children and young people in Scotland. In *V v. UK* and *T v. UK* (2000) 30 EHRR 121, the European Court of Human Rights found the UK to be in breach of Article 6 (the right to a fair trial) in the case of Thomson and Venables (the children who were tried in an adult court in England for the murder of James Bulger). The court held that children should be treated in a manner that takes into account their age, maturity and understanding, in order to have a fair trial. Court proceedings should be less formal and attempts should be made to ensure that the child understands what is going on.

When the Scottish Executive announced the youth court pilot scheme, this was welcomed by some commentators as an opportunity to improve the criminal process as it relates to children (albeit just persistent offenders aged 16–17) and some even suggested that its remit could be extended to include 21 year olds in the future, creating a separate youth justice process (Whyte, 2004). Activity 35 allows you to examine the youth court pilot scheme and consider how attendance at a criminal court affects children and young people.

Allow about 1 hour
30 minutes

## Activity 35   Youth court pilots and the experiences of children in court

Website

Following the link from this activity on the course website, read the journal article 'The Politicization of Youth Crime in Scotland and the Rise of the "Burberry Court"'. This article contains a strong critique of the youth court pilots in Scotland and the experiences of children within an adult criminal process. Make notes in answer to the following questions:

1   What are the aims of the youth court pilots and where are they based?

2   Why do the authors question the legality of separate courts for persistent offenders?

3   What are the differences between the youth court and the adult sheriff court?

4   How do the young people involved experience the court process? Do they seem to understand it?

5   What is the role of the social worker in this process?

## Comment

This article clearly highlights the controversy that surrounds the reintroduction of a youth court model in Scotland and the policy context of current youth justice reforms. Piacentini and Walters argue that the hopes for a more welfare-oriented justice process have not been borne out in an initiative that was founded on fast-tracking persistent offenders. They identify the possibility of a human rights challenge to these arrangements because the criteria for referral to the youth court (persistent offending) have the potential to prejudice a criminal trial (where due process demands that the offender is presumed to be innocent and the judge has no knowledge of their previous convictions).

Regardless of whether the youth court pilots are extended or adopted in their present form, the observations made of the children's experience in the courtroom are instructive. They demonstrate how court proceedings and the courtroom environment can isolate and confuse young people. This is starkly different to the informalism of the children's hearings setting that they had previously experienced and is not conducive to consideration of the child's best interests or rights. For example, the authors note that none of the young people were invited to provide input into the youth court proceedings. These findings suggest serious shortcomings in prosecuting children and young people within the adult courts.

Social workers have an important role to play in supporting children and young people who come to court and helping them to understand the process. In this case, for example, those interviewed did not appear to appreciate that the powers of the youth court were the same as the adult sheriff court and therefore underestimated the seriousness of their predicament. The aim of the youth court was to have dedicated youth court social workers who were familiar with the range of possible disposals, additional services and specific obligations in relation to children and young people. In practice this was not always possible.

### Children subject to detention

Offenders under 21 years of age cannot be sentenced to detention unless the sentencing judge is of the opinion that no other sentence is appropriate. The type of detention applied, however, will depend on the age of the offender and the procedure by which they were prosecuted (summary or solemn).

In extremely serious cases a child may be liable to prosecution by the solemn procedure, although such cases are rare. Section 208 of the Criminal Procedure (Scotland) Act 1995 makes provision for the detention of children in these cases:

> Where a child is convicted on indictment and the court is of the opinion that no other method of dealing with him is appropriate, it may sentence him to be detained for such a period which it shall specify in the sentence; and the child shall during that period be liable to be detained in such place and on such conditions as the Secretary of State may direct.

The wording of section 208 allows that the place need not be a penal institution. Where the child is under the age of 16 this may be in secure care and where the offender is aged 16–20 detention will be in a young offender institution. No one under the age of 21 can be sent to prison.

Where a person under the age of 18 is convicted of murder, he must be sentenced to be detained 'without limit of time', and detained in a place and conditions determined by the Scottish ministers (s. 205 (2)). Where this takes them beyond their 21st birthday they will be transferred from a young offender institution to prison.

For all other cases release is governed by section 208. At the time of writing, short-term sentences of less than four years are subject to automatic release at the half-way point on licence. Long-term sentences are subject to release at the two-thirds point. A child can be released on licence at the recommendation of the Parole Board at any time and is subject to recall until the end of their sentence. (These provisions will be affected by the Custodial Sentences and Weapons (Scotland) Bill 2006, if enacted.)

When children are prosecuted on summary procedure, they appear before a sheriff court (and never a district court). Here a specific terminology applies: the words 'conviction' or 'sentence' must not be used in relation to children dealt with summarily. Instead 'a person found guilty of an offence' or 'a finding of guilt' or 'an order made upon such a finding' are used (s. 65 of the Criminal Procedure (Scotland) Act 1995). One of the disposals open to the court where the child is under 16 is to order a period of residential care. The period may not exceed one year, and must be of a specified length within that span. At the time of writing this is longer than the maximum power of detention available to the sheriff summary court. An order for residential care made under section 44 of the Criminal Procedure (Scotland) Act 1995 is subject to review by the local authority who, having regard to the child's best interests, may release them into the community, conditionally or unconditionally. The Parole Board is not involved in determining the release of children held under section 44 orders. The use of a section 44 order is the only means by which a child appearing before a court on summary procedure can be detained, but it is not necessarily a guarantee that detention will be in a particular institution. This is because it is up to the local authority in these cases to select the appropriate accommodation.

If placed in residential care, a child must be released not later than one-half of the specified period. They then remain on supervision as defined by the 1968 Act until the full period has elapsed, subject to review by the local authority at any time. Release of detained children normally involves assessment of the dual criteria of the best interests of the child and the protection of the public.

Sixteen to 17 year olds are particularly at risk of detention in a young offender institution, for the reasons stated earlier. In 2004/5 on an average day 560 young offenders were held in the two young offender institutions in Scotland (young women in YOI Cornton Vale, young men in YOI Polmont). Partly due to the development of diversionary strategies and non-custodial disposals, the overall number of young people in custody has been falling in recent years. This is to be welcomed because there is considerable evidence that community sanctions are more likely to reduce reoffending by this age group than their detention. It is important not to become complacent, however, as the statistics mask a significant increase in the number of young women detained in custody and there is a lack of alternative disposals for this age group. Social workers have a role in these institutions offering throughcare, contributing to the development of prison regimes and programmes that address offending behaviour.

Her Majesty's Chief Inspector of Prisons for Scotland has highlighted the continued practice of sending children under the age of 16 to young offender institutions on 'unruly certificates' (children who have not been accepted into secure care because of their behaviour). In 2005/6, 24 children aged 14–16 were held in prison, a practice described as 'shameful':

> These children are usually the least well-equipped for useful, happy, well-adjusted living. Most of them will have avoided school for years, they will have been victims of abuse, they will have bad physical and mental health and they will often have no-one who really cares for them. Prison is no place for a child. Nearly everyone agrees with that. Yet nothing changes.
>
> (McLellan, 2006)

## 3.9 Conclusion

Currently children and young people who have committed offences can end up in either the children's hearings system or the adult criminal justice process. These systems traditionally have different characteristics, although since devolution there has been a degree of convergence in their aims and the types of disposals available.

Social work services are central to youth justice in Scotland. The social work role and the legal framework that governs offence-based referrals to the children's hearings system have both been strengthened in recent years. There remains, however, a significant rate of detention of 16–21 year olds, which has given rise to concern that the criminal justice process, and social work involvement, is failing this age group.

An understanding of the legal framework, and a recognition of the importance of children's rights in this area, is essential to good social work practice. Social workers should promote children's rights and maximise the opportunities for diversion from the criminal justice process where this is appropriate.

## Key points

- There is no separate youth justice process in Scotland. The children's hearings system and criminal justice process operate in parallel.
- The age of criminal responsibility in Scotland is very low (8 years).
- The UNCRC contains specific provisions in relation to youth justice.
- Youth crime and justice has become a focus of policy and legislative developments in Scotland, particularly in relation to persistent young offenders.
- Youth justice teams are responsible for the delivery of social work services for children and young people referred on offence grounds to the children's hearing system.
- National Standards for Youth Justice Services set objectives and standards for practice.
- Many young people aged 16 or 17 who are charged with a criminal offence end up in an adult court and are the responsibility of criminal justice social work.
- The adult criminal justice system is not well suited to children and young people.

# 4 Mental disorder and criminal justice

For this section you will need:
- course website access for online activities.

## Core questions

- What is the position of people with mental disorders who come into contact with the criminal justice process?
- How can social workers provide effective support to these service users?
- What is the role of an appropriate adult?
- What is the role of the social worker in managing the risks posed by some mentally disordered offenders and supporting them in the community?

## 4.1 Introduction

The final section of this block provides an introduction to the particular needs of people suffering from mental disorder who come into contact with the criminal justice process and the special arrangements that exist in relation to this group. In many instances the processes involved in dealing with and disposing of cases where a person is deemed to be suffering from a mental disorder will not include social workers. The police, procurators fiscal, courts and medical authorities are the primary points of referral. The role of mental health officers (specialist social workers with particular powers under mental health legislation) is also important, but will not be covered here, as the primary aim is to inform criminal justice social workers and generic practitioners who are working within the criminal justice process. (The social work role and legal framework in relation to mental health and adults with incapacity is covered in Block 4.)

Criminal justice social workers will encounter service users who are suffering from mental disorder and need to be able to recognise the symptoms of possible mental disorder as under-detection remains a significant problem in this area. They also need to understand the options that are available within the legal framework in order to effectively support service users. This is a complex area of practice because it involves familiarity with two legal systems: criminal justice and mental health. It is also an area where there are sometimes conflicting policy concerns that can impact on decision making and create dilemmas for social workers. While policy continues to encourage and emphasise the importance of diverting the mentally disordered to appropriate care and treatment, recent preoccupations with risk – fuelled by a number of widely publicised homicides in England in the 1990s involving individuals with mental health problems – have contributed to a growing equation in the public mind of mental illness and dangerousness. Though the impact of these developments on policy and legislation has been more muted in Scotland than in England and Wales, the shift towards a 'public safety' or risk management agenda is now evident in the criminal justice process's response to mentally disordered offenders.

## 4.2 Mental disorder and crime

We will start by considering public perceptions of the relationship between mental disorder and crime.

Allow about 20 minutes

### Activity 36   Who is the mentally disordered offender?

Write down any words, phrases or images that come to mind when you hear the term 'mentally disordered offender'. You may find it helpful to ask a family member, friend or colleague for their response to this term. After you have made some notes, spend a few minutes thinking about whether the description that you have compiled is an accurate and/or fair representation of the mentally disordered people who come into contact with the criminal justice process.

### Comment

A common response to this kind of activity is a list of infamous criminals who have committed serious violent and sexual offences. These 'monsters' are among the most feared for their unpredictable and seemingly irrational acts perpetrated against strangers. Their crimes prompt concerns about risk and public protection and in some cases highlight failures in professional decision making and the scope of legal powers. You may have noted the association of certain types of mental disorder with offending behaviour: paranoid schizophrenics and 'psychopaths' are often high on the list. Perhaps you also included some of the popular derogatory phrases that contribute to the stigma surrounding mental health issues, or simply described them as evil.

Thankfully these types of offences are rare, but when they do happen they are not the sole province of the mentally disordered. In fact this is not an accurate reflection of the mentally disordered in the criminal justice process at all. What about the woman with post-natal depression who has smothered her child? Or the teenager with Down's syndrome who indulges in inappropriate sexual touching? All have forms of mental disorder and commit crimes of sex and violence, but they raise some difficult issues in relation to the justice of a criminal response. You may wish to define these acts differently. Are they 'crimes'? Are the actors responsible criminals? Should we punish them or divert and excuse?

Research consistently shows that when people with mental disorder offend they are more likely to commit minor property offences or acts of an antisocial nature. If they are violent or harmful, that tendency is frequently focused on themselves, rather than others (rates of suicide and self harm are high) (Peay, 2002).

Mental disorder is defined in section 227 of the Mental Health (Care and Treatment) (Scotland) Act 2003 as including those with a mental illness, personality disorder or learning disability. There is, however, no legal definition of the term 'mentally disordered offender', although this phrase is used liberally in policy documents and guidance frameworks for the provision of services. There is a growing awareness that this is a problematic description for a diverse range of potential service users. For example, the phrase mentally disordered offenders suggests a necessary connection between mental disorder and crime, where this may not exist. A person may have the disorder before they commit a crime, or develop it after and there may be no causal connection between the two.

You will remember from Activity 2 that the term 'offender' should also be used with caution. The mentally disordered individuals who come to the attention of the police are not automatically offenders. Even where a harmful act has been committed they may be diverted from the criminal justice process without prosecution, or if prosecuted will not be found guilty if their mental disorder provides a defence to the criminal charge.

An analysis of the complex relationship between mental disorder and crime goes beyond the scope of this section. It is, however, relevant to the assessment of individuals in both the health and criminal justice contexts. Social workers should be alert to the possibility of discrimination in this area, as perceptions of the 'mentally disordered offender' have the potential to shape responses to this group. The labels mentally disordered and offenders are categories to which stigma is attached. When combined they can obscure other differences that will often be more important, such as a person's social circumstances, their substance misuse and other factors that can influence behaviour.

> [M]entally disordered offenders are first and foremost people; whether they may have offended or whether they may be disordered will be matters for individual resolution. Prioritization of one aspect (the mentally disordered element) of an individual's make-up readily leads to neglect of other, perhaps more pertinent, aspects. Mentally disordered people may have other needs which are arguably as important in respect of their special status within the criminal justice system.
>
> (Peay, 2002, p. 752)

Guidance to health, social work and related services for mentally disordered offenders in Scotland similarly emphasises the importance of seeing the individual and respecting their rights:

> The mentally disordered offender is an individual who is entitled to treatment of his or her underlying condition and respect of their rights, as is any other individual. ... A variety of social and clinical facilities and treatments will be required within different settings and with varying levels of security so that the individual may be appropriately placed. Depending on the needs of the individual some of these facilities will be in hospital, some in prison and some in the community.
>
> (Scottish Office, 1999, para. 1.11)

Social care services have an important role in meeting this value commitment. They should recognise that individuals will not always accept the medicalisation of the reasons for their offending behaviour and may reject offers of treatment or diversion as a result.

## 4.3 Diversion and the two-system approach

Policy in respect of mentally disordered offenders is based on the premise that they should receive care and treatment from health and social services and, where appropriate, be diverted from contact with the criminal justice system at an early stage. The mental health system is therefore engaged to provide services in parallel with agencies of criminal justice. They should:

> Provide care under conditions of appropriate (but no greater than necessary) security with due regard for public safety
>
> Have regard to quality of care and proper attention to the needs of individuals

Where possible, provide care in the community rather than in institutions

Provide care that maximises rehabilitation and the individual's chance of an independent life.

(Scottish Office (1999), quoted in SPICe, 1999, p. 2)

The law provides a series of opportunities for diversion to health assessment and treatment throughout the criminal justice process, as illustrated in Figure 13.

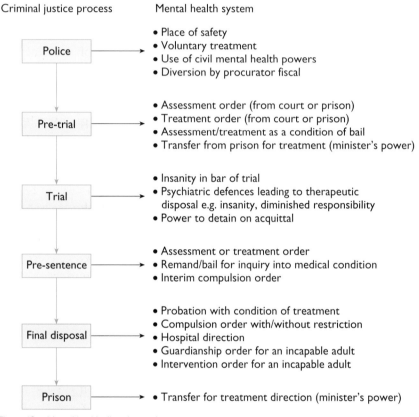

Figure 13   Mental health diversion pathways

These diversion pathways are provided within two key pieces of legislation that are important reference points when working with this group:

• Mental Health (Care and Treatment) (Scotland) Act 2003 (civil and criminal provisions)

• Criminal Procedure (Scotland) Act 1995.

The Mental Health (Care and Treatment) (Scotland) Act 2003 is underpinned by key principles that determine its use (see Block 4, Section 4). Criminal justice social workers need to be aware of the opportunities for diversion that exist within the legal framework, although they are not expected to be experts in this field.

You will see from what follows that the various options for diversion are subject to different criteria and have different consequences. For example, diversion by the procurator fiscal may lead to the cessation of criminal proceedings, but other forms of diversion, on a voluntary or compulsory basis (such as a court order for assessment), will not necessarily prevent the criminal process from continuing. Some court ordered disposals require the consent of the offender (e.g. a probation order with a condition of treatment), but others do not (e.g. a treatment order). There are also different definitions of mental disorder in operation. Most of the civil and criminal powers available to the court use the wide definition of mental disorder in the Mental Health (Care and Treatment) (Scotland) Act 2003, but insanity in bar of trial (where an accused is found to be unfit to plead) and the psychiatric defences (such as insanity) employ much more restrictive definitions.

Research into the use of diversion pathways suggests that certain categories of mental disorder and types of people are less likely to be diverted from the criminal justice process than others (for a research summary see Atkinson et al., 2005). People with personality disorders, for example, can display many of the symptoms of mental illness, but may not meet the criteria for a clear diagnosis, and their condition can go unrecognised as a result. These people often do not respond to medical treatment and therefore, if they have offended, the responsibility to work with this group often falls to criminal justice social work. Depending on the type of personality disorder they can be difficult offenders to engage in the process of supervision and may need specially tailored programmes. Antisocial personality disorders, for example, are associated with violent behaviour and therefore this group is at particular risk of custody. It should be noted that the use of 'ordinary' criminal justice disposals can also be influenced by the presence of a mental disorder, for example those with severe antisocial personality disorder are more likely to receive an order for lifelong restriction than other violent offenders.

Social workers writing social enquiry reports (SERs) have an opportunity to secure access to assessment of mental disorder (e.g. by recommending adjournment for medical reports), and to ensure that the mentally disordered are not drawn into high-end punitive disposals on discriminatory grounds. For example, research suggests that African Caribbean men are more likely to receive police attention, be diagnosed with schizophrenia, assessed as at high risk of violence and drawn into the prison system (Riordan et al., 2004). Social workers should also be aware of a gender bias that operates in the opposite direction. Women coming into contact with the criminal justice process are more likely to be labelled as 'mad' and not 'bad' and be diverted as a result. This pathologising of women's offending is equally discriminatory and can have a damaging effect on their lives, leading for example to long-term restrictions of liberty in the mental health system.

A commitment to social work values is therefore essential to effective and ethical social work practice in this area.

## 4.4 Police contact

In a significant proportion of cases the first time that a person with mental disorder comes to the attention of health and social care services will be after an initial contact with the police. The behaviour exhibited by some mentally disordered individuals makes encounters with this entry point of the criminal justice process more likely, and the interpretation that the police place on this behaviour (as people in need of care or protection, or risky suspects in need of formal action) is of central importance. Police have formal powers under mental health legislation that enable them to detain for up to 24 hours individuals found in a public place if they are in immediate need of care and treatment, in order to take them to a 'place of safety' (Mental Health (Care and Treatment) Act 2003, section 297). Alternatively, if a crime is suspected they may arrest and/or detain the individual within ordinary police powers.

The mentally disordered are particularly vulnerable to criminalisation where their health condition goes undiagnosed on first police contact. In certain circumstances their mental disorder may lead to further vulnerability in the police station, where for example they may be at risk of self-harm in custody or be suggestible under interview. Vulnerable adults (for example those suffering from mental illness or with a learning disability) may also have communication problems that result in them giving misleading statements. They can misunderstand what is happening to them and may be confused about the events that lead up to interview. For this reason certain safeguards apply. The police must assess the fitness of detainees for custody and interview and should consider the need for psychiatric assessment and treatment in conjunction with health services at the police station (e.g. forensic medical examiners). In a speech given at the launch of the guidance for police on interviewing people with mental disorders, the Scottish Office minister Henry McLeish said:

> We are committed to ensuring that someone who is being interviewed by the police is in the same position as anyone else. That means ensuring that the person is supported by an 'appropriate adult': someone independent of the police and the person who understands the needs of those with mental disorders and who can therefore help the person understand the implications of the procedures and the police understand the replies given.
>
> It is important that the police take special care when interviewing people – either as witnesses or suspects – with a mental disorder. Such people can, of course, be very capable of providing reliable evidence to the police, but they may have difficulty in fully understanding what is being said to them.
>
> (Scottish Office and Health Department, 1998)

Activity 37 helps you to understand the arrangements that can be made to assist vulnerable adults caught up in these circumstances.

---

Allow about 25 minutes     ## Activity 37   Appropriate adult schemes

Website

Following the link from this activity on the course website, read the research findings 'An Evaluation of Appropriate Adult Schemes in Scotland' and make notes in answer to the following questions:

1    What is the purpose of appropriate adult schemes?

2    In what circumstances should an investigating police officer consider involving an appropriate adult?

3    Who can act as an appropriate adult?

4    What is the role of the appropriate adult?

## Comment

The purpose of appropriate adult schemes is to ensure that whenever someone with a mental disorder is interviewed by the police, that person is provided with assistance by someone who is skilled in working with mentally disordered people, and who, because of their expertise, can facilitate the interview. Such people are known as appropriate adults. In Scotland (unlike England and Wales) the use of appropriate adults is not a statutory requirement, but failure to use one may result in a court refusing to admit evidence obtained in an interview on the grounds of fairness to the accused.

If a police officer is planning to start an interview and observes that the interviewee seems to be excessively anxious, is unable to make him or herself understood, is unable to answer or understand questions or is exhibiting unusual behaviour, the officer may ask for a medical opinion as to whether or not the person can be interviewed. The doctor or psychiatrist may offer an opinion that an appropriate adult should be called in – or the interviewing officer may decide from his or her own observations that such a step should be taken.

The appropriate adult should be someone who is completely independent of both the police and the person being interviewed and who has considerable experience of dealing with people who are suffering from mental disorder. In the majority of cases this will be a social worker employed by the local authority or a voluntary agency, but it could also be someone without a professional qualification who has the required knowledge and skills. Where the appropriate adult is a social worker, however, this report recommends that they should not act for known clients to avoid any confusion by the service user or appropriate adult about their role.

The role of the appropriate adult is to be on hand to provide support and reassurance to the person being interviewed and to facilitate communication between that person and the interviewer. The appropriate adult should also ensure that the person being interviewed by the police:

- is not disadvantaged in any way by virtue of the mental disorder from which they are suffering
- understands the procedures being applied
- understands the reasons for the interview
- fully understands the implications of any replies they might make.

The appropriate adult is not there to advise the person being interviewed as to how they should answer questions nor to object to the questions being asked. They might, of course, intervene in order to clarify misunderstandings or to facilitate communication.

There is also a role for the appropriate adult in court proceedings. A visit to the court beforehand accompanied by an appropriate adult might help the vulnerable person to deal with anxieties. However, it will be up to individual schemes to decide if an appropriate adult will be permitted to be present in court to offer reassurance and support during the process of a case.

---

The establishment of appropriate adult schemes is not just the responsibility of the police. These schemes are set up on an interdisciplinary basis with collaboration from the health and social work services as well as the voluntary sector and the police. It will be for the agencies involved to decide which will be the lead agency and this may vary according to local circumstances. However, it is suggested that social work departments should take the initiative in bringing together the relevant agencies. (Where they are the lead agency this responsibility is often sited within criminal justice services.)

## 4.5 Court processes

Where the charge is minor and a mental disorder is present the procurator fiscal may decide that it is not in the public interest to continue with the case. The procurator fiscal is also a point of referral to assessment and treatment, but this can only happen on a voluntary basis unless the accused meets the criteria for civil mental health powers or this is ordered by a criminal court. It is the procurator fiscal's duty to bring information about the presence of a mental disorder to the attention of the court, and they may be aided in this by psychiatric reports and/or contact with social work services.

In some areas multi-agency psychiatric liaison schemes are available to provide prompt access to mental health services within the court setting. When faced with someone who may have a mental disorder the court may require help in a number of areas (Moore and Whyte, 1998, p. 334):

- assessing the fitness of the accused person to plead to the charge

- assessing the state of mind of the accused person when the offence was committed, and

- deciding upon an appropriate disposal of the case.

The options available to the court are outlined in the mental health diversion pathway diagram in Figure 13, Section 4.3.

You are not expected to have a detailed understanding of all of the possible options as responsibility for legal advice on these issues rests with the accused's solicitor. Local authority social workers should consult colleagues with responsibility for adult care and providing services to children with mental health needs, for example mental health officers, where appropriate. In order to support these service users within the court process, however, criminal justice social workers need to have an overview of the process and be able to refer service users to further advice where necessary. Useful sources of information for this purpose are included in Box 32.

---

**Box 32 Guidance materials for best practice with mentally disordered offenders**

Volume 3 of the Mental Health (Care and Treatment) Scotland Act 2003 Code of Practice provides guidance for practitioners on the compulsory powers in relation to mentally disordered offenders.

The Scottish Executive has also produced an accessible topic guide for service users and carers: 'The New Mental Health Act – A guide for people involved in criminal justice proceedings'.

Both publications contain useful flow diagrams and are available on the Health and Community Care area of the Scottish Executive website (www).

---

It is important to remember that these options are in addition to the other possible criminal justice disposals that were studied in Section 2 of this block. Therapeutic disposals will not always be suitable, even where the accused is suspected of having or has a diagnosis of mental disorder. The threshold of compulsory intervention is set at a high level in order to respect individual autonomy and when met, remains subject to legislative principles that aim to respect the interests of the patient. For example, the use of powers under mental health legislation must provide maximum benefit to the patient and involve the minimum restriction on their freedom that is necessary in the circumstances. All of the options available are based on criteria that relate either to the person being a significant risk to their own health, safety or welfare or to the safety of others. Some are also dependent on resources being available in appropriate conditions of security to protect the public.

The following orders are in need of further explanation.

### Assessment order (s. 52B-J Criminal Procedure (Scotland) Act 1995)

An assessment order can be applied for by the prosecutor, Scottish ministers, or the court. Where an individual meets the appropriate grounds, an assessment order authorises the detainment of the individual in hospital for up to 28 days. This will normally involve a period of assessment, culminating in the provision of reports to the court by a responsible medical officer (RMO) and a mental health officer (MHO) who will investigate the person's social circumstances. The following issues would normally be addressed within the reports:

- insanity in bar (at the time) of trial
- insanity at time of offence
- diminished responsibility
- appropriate disposals.

An assessment order may also involve a period of treatment but only if an approved medical practitioner (AMP) identifies that this is in the best interest of the patient.

### Treatment order (s. 52K-S Criminal Procedure (Scotland) Act 1995)

A treatment order can be made while an individual is awaiting trial or sentence and can be applied for by the prosecutor (prior to conviction), Scottish ministers (while awaiting trial or sentence) or the court. Again, subject to the appropriate grounds being met, a treatment order authorises the detainment of an individual in hospital for a period of medical treatment. The order lasts until the case is concluded. As with the assessment order an RMO must report to the court on the same issues as outlined above for an assessment order. If the accused is found to be insane the court may order a therapeutic disposal (either with or without restriction to hospital). In high risk cases the court must order a compulsion order with restrictions.

### Compulsion orders (interim s. 53 or final disposal with/without restriction s. 57 Criminal Procedure (Scotland) Act 1995)

A compulsion order can be based either in the community or within hospital and involves a period of compulsory treatment as justified under the Mental Health (Care and Treatment) (Scotland) Act 2003. It is available following conviction for an offence punishable with imprisonment (where the sentence is not fixed by law). An interim compulsion order can be used before sentence for in-patient assessment if the court is considering a compulsion order as a final disposal.

If the offender poses a particular risk of serious harm to others a restriction order can be added to a compulsion order, allowing for the offender to be detained in hospital without limit of time.

### Guardianship order (s. 58(1A) Criminal Procedure (Scotland) Act 1995)

Where an incapable adult meets the criteria of the Adults with Incapacity (Scotland) Act 2000, a guardianship order can be made. It can be ordered on welfare grounds in criminal proceedings following conviction for an offence punishable with imprisonment (where the sentence is not fixed by law) or following acquittal on grounds of insanity. This allows for the appointment of a welfare guardian who will be given powers considered necessary in relation to the incapable adult's particular needs. A guardianship order does not authorise compulsory treatment. It enables welfare needs to be met within a community or residential care setting.

### Hospital direction (s. 59A Criminal Procedure (Scotland) Act 1995)

This is a hybrid order allowing for detention in hospital in conjunction with a prison sentence. The patient remains restricted to hospital as long as the sentence lasts and if they no longer require treatment will be returned to prison. A hospital direction is only available after conviction on indictment of an offence punishable with imprisonment, where the offender poses a risk of serious harm to others.

Activity 38 allows you to consider the application of these orders.

---

Allow about 40 minutes

## Activity 38   Options available to the court

Read this case study and, with reference to Figure 13 'Mental health diversion pathways' in Section 4.3, make notes on the questions that follow.

> Ronald is a 50-year-old man with a learning disability and a previous diagnosis of schizophrenia. Following a sexual assault on a neighbour Ronald appeared before the court. Ronald has lived for most of his life in institutions. He was discharged to a supported flat five years ago and appeared to have settled well. The neighbour is a young woman who provided informal care in that she would bring Ronald milk and a newspaper in the morning. Since the assault the victim has been living with relatives and she is frightened to return home. She has been receiving treatment from her GP for depression and anxiety, and she is unable to return to work. Ronald was detained in hospital for assessment following the assault. He is confused and says he did nothing wrong. He describes the assault as his response to a hug from his neighbour. He doesn't like the hospital and he wants to go home.

1   What options are available to the court?

2   What do you think would be an appropriate course of action, and why?

3   Would social work have a role in this process?

4   What are Ronald's rights in this situation?

5   What are the victim's rights in this situation?

## Comment

If, as is likely, the psychiatric assessment concluded that Ronald had a mental disorder and the further legislative criteria were met, the court could apply any of the above orders. The decision would rest on the procurator fiscal as to the court process to be applied (summary or solemn), the court's view of the severity of the offence and the risk Ronald was perceived to present to the community. This is a serious offence and Ronald demonstrates no understanding of this. He does not accept any responsibility or show any remorse, and as a result he could be deemed to present some risk to the community. On this basis, the court could impose a compulsion order, possibly with restriction.

Prior to making an order the court may seek background information by means of an SER. Ronald's learning disability may affect his ability to fully participate in this assessment and to understand the consequences of any possible court action. The social worker should be sensitive to his needs and facilitate this, if necessary by engaging advocacy services. It may also be appropriate for the social worker in Ronald's case to be male.

The social worker preparing the report has a responsibility to seek credible alternatives to custody for the court. The social worker could take the view that the level of risk is unlikely to be managed in the community in the short term and could highlight alternative mental health disposals. In a serious case such as this, the criminal justice social work role is unlikely to extend beyond the preparation of an SER. If Ronald were sentenced to imprisonment, however, they would have throughcare responsibilities in his case and would need to ensure that his mental health needs were recognised in custody.

Ronald has the right to appeal against any sentence.

If a pilot scheme is in place the victim could make a written statement to the court outlining the impact the crime has had on them (section 14 Criminal Justice (Scotland) Act 2003). If Ronald was sent to prison this Act would also entitle his victim to notification of his release, but where a community or mental health disposal is ordered she has no equivalent rights.

## 4.6 The social work role and tasks

The social worker will have a role in terms of the four community-based disposals that are available to the court.

### Community-based compulsion order

This is as detailed above.

### Supervision and treatment order

This can be imposed for any crime (except murder) where the accused person has been found unfit to plead and has been found to have committed the act with which they were charged. There have to be two medical reports saying that the accused's condition requires treatment but does not necessitate a hospital order. In addition, there have to be arrangements in place for the treatment component of the order. The order requires the person to be under the supervision of a social worker for a specified period, which cannot exceed three years. The order has three conditions. The 'supervised person' must:

1  keep in touch with the supervising officer and notify him or her of any change of address
2  comply with the instructions of the supervising officer
3  submit to treatment with a view to the improvement of their medical condition.

*Guardianship order*

Described above. In criminal cases the guardian must be the local authority or someone appointed by them. A social worker may therefore be appointed to act as guardian or have a supervisory role.

*Probation*

There is a special provision in the Criminal Procedure (Scotland) Act 1995 that requires treatment of a mental condition as part of a probation order. The order places the person under the supervision of a social worker and under the direction of a medical practitioner or a psychologist. Such an order will require that there be good liaison between the professionals involved so that a coherent plan of work is maintained. It should be noted that such a condition does not permit treatment to be given without the consent of the offender, but if the offender refuses treatment, he or she would be in breach of probation.

Only probation would directly involve criminal justice social work supervision.

Allow about 45 minutes

### Activity 39   Janine's case

Read the case study below and, with reference to Figure 13 'Mental health diversion pathways' in Section 4.3, make notes on the questions that follow.

> Janine is a 26-year-old woman with a history of shoplifting and other theft offences. She has an extensive history of drug misuse and her previous offences have all been related to this as she was stealing to gain funds to buy drugs. Janine has been subject to a number of disposals, including probation, but never custody. Following her conviction on a breach of the peace and a minor assault charge, the court has asked for an SER.
>
> During your interview with Janine, she discloses that at the time of the offence and on other occasions she could hear people discussing what she was thinking, and making disparaging remarks about her. She cannot see the people but she can hear them and she thinks that everyone else can. On the day of the offence she admits to shouting at people around her to be quiet. This was to enable her to ascertain the source of these voices. One person refused to be quiet and Janine tried to cover this person's mouth; this resulted in a scuffle. Janine acknowledges that she was using drugs at the time and that she continues to do so. She also informs you that she has previously sought help at the local psychiatric hospital. She says that on these occasions she has been interviewed and sent home, as she was considered to be drug seeking. On one occasion she was considered to be experiencing a drug-induced psychosis and as a result she was kept in hospital overnight and discharged the following day. The court has asked for a psychiatric assessment and Janine has now been diagnosed with schizophrenia.

1 What options are available to the court?

2 What would be your advice to the court? Give your reasons.

3 What are Janine's rights in this situation?

## Comment

The court has a number of options available: they could sentence Janine under their criminal justice powers or consider a diversion to psychiatric treatment. Dual diagnosis cases (where the offender is exhibiting signs of mental illness and drug use) are difficult to assess and to treat, although her current offence does appear to be related to her diagnosis of schizophrenia.

Janine has previously sought help and seems willing to engage with psychiatric services. It would therefore seem unnecessary to impose a compulsion order. Her previous record, however, is likely to sway the sentencing judge towards a criminal justice disposal and although her present offence is not serious she may be at risk of custody. The social worker has a role to inform the court of the alternative non-custodial options. They should also promote anti-discriminatory practice by conducting a risk assessment and highlighting the ways in which schizophrenia can be successfully managed in the community.

Janine's compliance with the treatment of her condition could be monitored on probation, and this could be a condition of a probation order. If Janine is motivated to address her drug use the social worker could also ask for an additional condition that Janine attend drug counselling as directed by her supervising officer. A drug treatment and testing order could also be considered to monitor her compliance with this condition. The social worker would then advise the court of any failure to comply by means of standard breach procedures.

Janine must have probation explained to her. This must be done in court and it would be good practice for the social worker to do this in more detail at the SER interview. The social worker will also have to liaise with psychiatric services to ensure that appropriate arrangements can be made. Janine has to agree to be placed on probation and to any attached condition, although failure to do so is likely to result in a more restrictive disposal. She can appeal against any sentence.

The value of partnership should therefore be recognised when working with Janine and other agencies, while also acknowledging that there are tensions between care and control in the social work role.

---

Social workers also work with sentenced prisoners and as such should be aware of the minister's power to transfer a convicted prisoner to hospital for treatment (section 136 Mental Health (Care and Treatment) Act 2003). In practice the use of this provision is limited by of the number of places available in the secure hospital estate. Research shows that there is a very high incidence of mental disorder in prison and facilities are necessary to provide for its assessment and treatment within prison walls (Singleton et al., 1998; Myers, 2004). The establishment of mental health programmes and psychiatric in-reach services has led to an improvement in the conditions for this group, but these are not uniformly available. Social workers have a role in promoting these services in work with partner agencies, and their throughcare responsibilities are particularly important to ensure continuity of service provision to discharged mentally disordered prisoners.

## 4.7 Conclusion

This area of social work intervention is one in which the role of social workers is limited by the legislation and by the primacy of medical assessment and treatment and the decision of the courts. However, social workers have important tasks to perform in undertaking assessments, in providing supervision and support, and in liaising with other relevant professionals. The SER can convey important information to the courts to help them make informed decisions and in some instances can alert the court to potentially undetected mental health needs. Further supporting and sustaining people in the community and helping them to access appropriate services and treatment is another important social work role, as is supervising them on a formal basis.

Work with mentally disordered offenders is demanding and entails risk. The skills required to properly support the court and the offender are considerable, ranging from assessment and report-writing skills to accessing services on behalf of the offender.

### Key points

- The social worker has a key role in supporting people with a mental disorder who come into contact with the criminal justice process.
- Mentally disordered individuals may suffer from discrimination and can be particularly vulnerable in criminal justice settings.
- The role of the appropriate adult is to provide support and reassurance as well as to facilitate communication.
- Effective practice with mentally disordered offenders entails the ongoing assessment and management of risk.
- The social worker can support mentally disordered offenders in the community by supervising them and helping them to access services.

Allow about 1 hour

## 4.8 Consolidation activity

This activity requires you to consider the materials covered in this block and to identify the key social work responsibilities in relation to adult and youth offending. You will find it helpful to refer back to the flow diagrams in Figures 4 (Section 2.2), 8 (Section 2.3) and 10 (Sections 3.4) and to the relevant National Standards. Your answers should also demonstrate an understanding of how social work values are important for those working with offenders. Read the case study below and make notes in answer to the following questions.

> Patrick (37) and Iain (15) have been charged with robbery. They assaulted an elderly man and stole his wallet. The two were caught when purchasing clothes using the stolen chequebook and bank card.
>
> Patrick is the father of twins, aged 2. He is employed as a driver with a local taxi firm. His wife does not go out to work as she suffers from ill health and Patrick has the main responsibility for the children during the day, before working the night shift in his cab. This is not the first time Patrick has been convicted of an offence. Last year he served three months in prison for assault.

Iain is the son of one of Patrick's friends. He met Patrick at the local men's club where the two of them play snooker every Monday. Iain has been in trouble at school, mainly because of truanting. He spends his afternoons at Patrick's house because, he says, he cannot stand the constant fighting between his parents. Iain has a Saturday job at a local supermarket and he is the only person earning in his family. This is the first time he has been convicted of an offence.

1    How will Iain's case be treated differently from Patrick's in the early stages of the criminal justice process?

2    Given that Patrick pleads guilty to the charge of robbery, what happens next in the criminal justice process and how will social work be involved?

3    If you were asked to complete an SER for Patrick, how would you go about this and what information would you include in the report?

4    Given that Iain's case is referred to the children's reporter, what does this mean and how will social work be involved in the process?

5    If he is referred to the children's hearing on offence grounds, what support should be provided to Iain during this process and what might his action plan contain?

6    Describe what support social workers might be able to offer to Patrick and Iain's families.

7    What rights does the victim have in each case?

## Comment

Iain's age is important here as he is a child within the meaning of section 93(2)(b) of the Children (Scotland) Act 1995 and his best interests should be taken into account. Iain's welfare is paramount unless there is a risk of serious harm to the public. Children under the age of 16 will not be prosecuted unless they fall within the scope of the Lord Advocate's guidelines for joint reporting to the procurator fiscal (s. 42(1) Criminal Procedure (Scotland) Act 1995). While robbery is a serious offence, in this case the absence of a firearm or weapon would mean that he would not be subject to a trial on indictment. He would not, therefore, be reported with Patrick to the procurator fiscal. The police have discretion in how they would respond to Iain's behaviour. Because this is a first offence they could consider issuing a restorative warning, but given the seriousness of his actions and the presence of welfare concerns it is likely that he would be referred to the children's reporter.

With Patrick's previous offending record and the seriousness of the current offence it is most unlikely that he would be subject to diversion from prosecution at an early stage. Social work's first contact with Patrick would therefore be if they are requested to provide a SER to the sentencing court. This would be prepared by a criminal justice social worker.

If you were asked to prepare a SER in Patrick's case you would need to conduct further enquiries and interview Patrick in order to conduct a risk assessment and write a report. When writing the SER you would want to include the social and personal history of Patrick and something about his current circumstances. You would note the fact that Patrick plays a major part in caring for his two young children. The National Objectives and Standards for Social Work Services in the Criminal Justice System (NOS) (Scottish Executive, 2004d) state that information relevant to offending, particularly the offender's attitude to his behaviour, should be included in an SER. You would want to speak to Patrick in order to assess his feelings about what he did and comment in the report about any motivation to change.

Any history of criminal offences is also relevant, particularly when considering your recommendation to the court regarding sentence. You would need to make enquiries about whether Patrick has any other convictions besides the one for assault last year. In considering your recommendation you would take into account Patrick's income as well as his work and family responsibilities. There are a number of sentencing options available to the court and your report would have to include comment about the appropriateness of these and their impact on his family. You will remember that one of the social work objectives in the NOS is to achieve a reduction in the incidence of custody. Patrick is likely to be at risk of custody and your report should therefore contain a consideration of non-custodial options. You can remind yourself about these by referring to Table 3 on sentencing disposals in Section 2.5 of this block.

Although Patrick has been in custody before and will have been the subject of an SER in the past, it would be good practice to discuss the purpose of the report with him. After writing your report, Patrick should be given the opportunity to read it and to comment on the accuracy of the contents. He is entitled to retain a copy.

When Iain's case is referred to the children's reporter, inquiries will be made into the circumstances of his offence and family background. The reporter will request an assessment from social work services and a youth justice social worker or generic children and families' worker would have to write a report. This would involve talking to Iain and his family and obtaining further information, for example by speaking to his teachers. An assessment would be made of his offending behaviour but you would also note that there are additional welfare concerns. For example, it is clear that he is the only earner in his household, has been truanting from school and there are questions about the impact of his parent's relationship on his well-being.

You should remember that Iain might not know what to expect in his initial meeting with you and may view your questions as intrusive. You should explain to him what the report is and why it has been requested. This would include telling Iain why you are asking certain questions about him and his circumstances. Copies of the reports would normally be given to Iain and his parents and it is good practice to provide Iain with an opportunity to read this and comment on its contents.

The reporter has various options available to them. If Iain and his family were to voluntarily engage with social work services there may not be a referral to a hearing in this case. It would also be open to the reporter to refer the case to a hearing on grounds other than his offence (e.g. for truanting). If this were to happen no criminal conviction would be recorded against Iain. If he is referred to a hearing (on offence grounds or otherwise) the social worker should support him and his family through this process and explain the options available to the hearing. As Iain is not a persistent offender his action plan would not recommend an intensive offence-based programme. If Iain is placed on supervision the social worker would be able to work with him to address his awareness of the consequences of his offence and this might include a restorative justice element, such as writing a letter to his victim. It could be helpful to assist Iain in finding a group of young people with whom he can socialise, as well as speaking to his teachers about strategies for dealing with his truanting.

Part of the role of social workers in both the criminal justice and youth justice processes is to assist the families of offenders. The social worker would need to work with Iain's parents to encourage him back to school and attempt to address their parental responsibilities. The possibility of domestic violence in this relationship should also be considered, providing advice and support where appropriate. In Patrick's case his family will need support if he receives a custodial sentence

You should remember that in addition to the social work practice objectives within the legal framework, the values of partnership and empowerment should also be promoted.

Finally it is important to recognise the interests of the victim in this case. He should receive information and advice on the progress of the case against Patrick from the Victim Information and Advice service attached to the Crown Office and Procurator Fiscal Service (COPFS). If a pilot scheme is in operation he may also be able to provide a victim statement for consideration at the sentencing stage. In Iain's case responsibility for advising the victim of the process and informing him of any disposal rests with the children's reporter. He may also be invited to participate in any restorative justice response, but would not be required to do so.

# References

Adams, L. (2006) '£12m youth crime tagging branded a costly failure', *The Herald*, 18 August.

Anderson, S., Bromley, C. and Given, L. (2005) 'Public attitudes towards young people and youth crime in Scotland', *Research Findings*, no. 7, July 2005, Edinburgh, Scottish Executive.

Anderson, S., Ingram, D. and Hutton, N. (2002) 'Public attitudes towards sentencing and alternatives to imprisonment', *Scottish Parliament Paper*, no. 537, session 1, 2002, Edinburgh, HMSO.

Andrews, D.A. and Bonta, J.L. (1995) *The Level of Service Inventory – Revised Manual*, Toronto, Multi-Health Systems.

Andrews, D.A. et al. (1990) 'Does correctional treatment work? A clinically relevant and psychologically informed meta-analysis', *Criminology*, vol. 28, no. 3, pp. 369–404.

Association of Directors of Social Work in Scotland (ADSW) (1996a) *The Values and Principles and Social Work Practice in the Criminal Justice System*, Edinburgh, ADSW.

Association of Directors of Social Work in Scotland (ADSW) (1996b) *Policy Statement on Victims of Crime*, Edinburgh, ADSW, February.

Association of Directors of Social Work in Scotland (ADSW) (2003) *Policy Statement on Criminal Justice Social Work*, Edinburgh, ADSW, November.

Atkinson, J.M., Reilly, J., Garner, H. and Patterson, L. (2005) *Review of Literature Relating to Mental Health Legislation*, Scottish Executive Social Research, Edinburgh, Scottish Executive.

Audit Scotland (2001) *Youth Justice in Scotland: A Baseline Report*, Edinburgh, Audit Scotland.

Audit Scotland (2002) *Dealing with Offending by Young People*, Edinburgh, Audit Scotland.

Barry, M. (2000) 'The mentor/monitor debate in criminal justice: "what works" for offenders', *British Journal of Social Work*, vol. 30, p. 575.

Birch, A., Dobbie, F., Chalmers, T., Barnsdale, L. and McIvor, G. (2006) 'Evaluation of the arrest referral pilot schemes', *Research Findings*, no. 87/2006, Edinburgh, Scottish Executive.

Bonta, J.L. (1996) 'Risk-needs assessment and treatment' in Harland, A.J. (ed.) *Choosing Correctional Options That Work: Defining the Demand and Evaluating The Supply*, Thousand Oaks, CA, Sage.

Brown, L. and Levy, L. (1998) *Social Work and Criminal Justice: Volume 4 – Sentencer Decision Making*, Edinburgh, The Stationery Office.

Buist, M. (2005) *What Works with Children and Young People involved in Crime? A Review of Scottish Research*, Edinburgh, CJSW Development Centre for Scotland.

CCETSW (1996) 'Nothing works' (handout), *Teaching Criminal Justice Social Work on the DipSW*, Edinburgh, CCETSW.

Croall, H. (2005) 'Criminal justice in the devolved Scotland' in Mooney, G. and Scott, G. (eds) *Exploring Social Policy in the New Scotland*, Bristol, Policy Press.

Croall, H. (2006) 'Criminal justice in post-devolutionary Scotland', *Critical Social Policy*, vol. 26, no. 3, p. 587.

Crown Office and Procurator Fiscal Service (COPFS) (2005) *Prosecution Code*, Edinburgh, COPFS.

Crown Office and Procurator Fiscal Service (COPFS) (2006) *Lord Advocate's Guidelines to Chief Constables: Reporting to Procurators Fiscal of Offences Alleged to have been Committed by Children*, Edinburgh, COPFS.

Dutton, K. and Whyte, B. (2006) 'Implementing restorative justice within an integrated welfare system: evaluation of Glasgow's restorative justice service', *CJSW Briefing*, Edinburgh, Criminal Justice Social Work Development Centre for Scotland.

Fabb, J. and Guthrie, T.G. (1997) *Social Work and the Law in Scotland* (2nd edn), Edinburgh, Lexis Nexis UK.

Heery, G. (1996) 'Competence in criminal justice' in O'Hagan, K. (ed.) *Competence in Social Work Practice,* London, Jessica Kingsley, chapter 8.

Her Majesty's Chief Inspector of Prisons for Scotland (HMCIP) (2002) *Annual Report for 2002–3*, Edinburgh, The Stationery Office.

Houchin, R. (2005) *Social Exclusion and Imprisonment in Scotland*, Edinburgh, Scottish Prison Service.

Hutton, N. (1999) 'Sentencing in Scotland' in Duff, P. and Hutton, N. (eds) *Criminal Justice in Scotland*, Aldershot, Ashgate/Dartmouth.

Hutton, N. (2005) 'Beyond populist punitiveness', *Punishment and Society*, vol. 7, no. 3, pp. 243–58.

Justice Department (2001) *Criminal Justice Social Work Services: National Priorities for 2001–2002 and Onwards*, Edinburgh, Scottish Executive.

Keith, B. (2006) *Report of the Zahid Mubarek Inquiry*, London, The Stationery Office.

Kemshall, H. (1996) *Reviewing Risk*, London, Home Office Research and Statistics Directorate.

Kennedy, R. and McIvor, G. (1992) *Young Offenders in the Children's Hearing System and the Criminal Justice Systems: A Comparative Analysis*, Dundee, Tayside Regional Council/Social Work Research Centre.

Kilbrandon, C.S. (1964) *Report of the Committee on Children and Young Persons, Scotland*, Cmnd 2306, Edinburgh, HMSO (Kilbrandon Report).

Levy, G., Kemshall, H. and McIvor, G. (2002) *Serious Violent and Sexual Offenders: The Use of Assessment Tools in Scotland*, Edinburgh, Scottish Executive.

Lipsey, M.W. (1990) 'Juvenile development treatment: A meta-analytic enquiry into the variability of effects' in Cook, T.D. et al. (eds) *Meta-analysis for Explanation: A Casebook*, New York, Russell Sage Foundation.

Lloyd, C., Mair, G. and Hough, M. (1995) 'Explaining reconviction rates: A critical analysis', *Home Office Research Study*, no. 136, London, Home Office.

McAra, L. (2005) 'Modelling penal transformation', *Punishment and Society*, vol. 7, no. 3, pp. 277–302.

McAra, L. (2006) 'Welfare in crisis? Key developments in Scottish youth justice' in Muncie, J. and Goldson, B. (eds) *Comparative Youth Justice*, London, Sage.

McAra, L. and McVie, S. (2005) 'The usual suspects? Street-life, young people and the police', *Criminal Justice*, vol. 5, no. 1, p. 5–36.

McConnell, J. (2003) 'Respect, responsibility and rehabilitation in modern Scotland' [online], Apex Lecture, http://www.scottishexecutive.gov.uk/News/News-Extras/157 (Accessed 26 January 2007).

McCulloch, P. (2005) 'Probation, social context and desistance: Retracing the relationship', *Probation Journal*, vol. 52, no. 1, p. 8–22.

McGuire, J. and Priestley, P. (1995) 'Reviewing "what works": past, present and future' in McGuire, J. (ed.) *What Works: Reducing Reoffending – Guidelines from Research and Practice*, Chichester, Wiley.

McIvor, G. (2004) 'Getting personal: developments in policy and practice in Scotland' in Mair, G. (ed) *What Matters in Probation*, Collumpton, Willan.

McIvor, G. and Barry, M. (1998) *The Process and Outcomes of Community-based Throughcare*, Edinburgh, Central Research Unit, Scottish Office.

McLellan, A. (2006) 'I'll never get used to seeing children in prison', *The Herald*, 2 November.

McNeill, F. (2004) 'Desistance, rehabilitation and correctionalism: developments and prospects in Scotland', *The Howard Journal*, vol. 43, no. 4, pp. 420–36.

McNeill, F. (2005) 'Remembering probation in Scotland', *Probation Journal*, vol. 52, no. 1, pp. 23–38.

McNeill, F. and Batchelor, S. (2004) *Persistent Offending by Young People: Developing Practice*, London, National Association of Probation Officers (NAPO).

McNeill, F. and Whyte, B. (forthcoming) *Reducing Reoffending: Social Work and Community Justice in Scotland*, Cullompton, Willan.

McNeill, F., Batchelor, S., Burnett, R. and Knox, J. (2005) *21st Century Social Work Review, Reducing Reoffending: Key Practice Skills*, Edinburgh, The Scottish Executive.

Macpherson, W. (1999) *The Stephen Lawrence Inquiry: Report of an Inquiry by William Macpherson of Cluny et al.*, London, The Stationery Office (Macpherson Report).

May, C. (1999) 'Explaining reconviction following a community sentence: The role of social factors', *Home Office Research Study*, no. 192, London, Home Office.

Moore, G. and Whyte, B. (1998) *Social Work and the Criminal Law in Scotland*, Edinburgh, Mercat Press.

Myers, F. (2004) 'On the borderline? People with learning disabilities and/or autistic spectrum disorders in secure, forensic and other specialist settings', *Research Findings*, no. 39/2004, Edinburgh, Scottish Executive.

National Association for the Care and Resettlement of Offenders (NACRO) (2000) *Pre-Sentence Reports and Custodial Sentencing*, NACRO briefing, December, London, NACRO.

NCH Scotland (2004) *Where's Kilbrandon Now? Report and Recommendations from the Inquiry*, Glasgow, NCH.

New Zealand Ministry of Justice (2004) *Restorative Justice in New Zealand: Best Practice*, Wellington, Ministry of Justice.

Normand, A. (2003) *Criminal Justice System Objectives Review: Proposals for the Integration of Aims, Objectives and Targets in the Scottish Criminal Justice System*, Edinburgh, Scottish Executive (Normand Report).

Peay, J. (2002) 'Mentally disordered offenders, mental health and crime' in Maguire, M., Morgan, R. and Reiner, R. (eds) *The Oxford Handbook of Criminology* (3rd edn), Oxford, Oxford University Press.

Piacentini, L. and Walters, R. (2006) 'The politicization of youth crime in Scotland and the rise of the "Burberry Court"', *Youth Justice*, vol. 6, no. 1, p. 43.

Rex, S. (2001) 'Beyond cognitive-behaviouralism? Reflections on the effectiveness literature' in Bottoms, A., Gelsthorpe, L. and Rex, S. (eds) *Community Penalties: Change and Challenges*, Collumpton, Willan.

Rifkind, M. (1989) 'Penal policy: The way ahead', *Howard Journal*, vol. 28, no. 2, pp. 81–90.

Rioch, C. and Manson, S. (2006) 'Achieving good outcomes with parents within the youth justice sector', paper presented at the Youth Justice Network conference, March, by the National Parenting Development Project.

Riordan, S., Donaldson, S. and Humphreys, M. (2004) 'The imposition of restricted hospital orders: Potential effects of ethnic origin', *International Journal of Law and Psychiatry*, vol. 27, p. 171.

Scottish Children's Reporter Administration (SCRA) (2005) *Framework for Decision Making by Reporters*, Stirling, SCRA.

Scottish Executive (2000) *It's a Criminal Waste: Stop Youth Crime Now: Report of Advisory Group on Youth Crime*, Edinburgh, Scottish Executive.

Scottish Executive (2002a) *A Better Way: The Report of the Ministerial Group on Women's Offending*, Edinburgh, Scottish Executive.

Scottish Executive (2002b) *National Standards for Scotland's Youth Justice Services*, Edinburgh, Scottish Executive.

Scottish Executive (2004a) *Re:duce, Re:habilitate, Re:form: A Consultation on Reducing Reoffending in Scotland*, Edinburgh, Scottish Executive.

Scottish Executive (2004b) *Supporting Safer, Stronger Communities: Scotland's Criminal Justice Plan*, Edinburgh, Scottish Executive.

Scottish Executive (2004c) *National Objectives and Standards for Social Work Services in the Criminal Justice System: Standards General Issues*, Edinburgh, Scottish Executive.

Scottish Executive (2004d) *National Objectives and Standards for Social Work Services in the Criminal Justice System: Standards Social Enquiry Reports and Associated Court Services*, Edinburgh, Scottish Executive.

Scottish Executive (2004e) *National Objectives and Standards for Social Work Services in the Criminal Justice System: Standards Throughcare*, Edinburgh, Scottish Executive

Scottish Executive (2004f) *National Objectives and Standards for Social Work Services in the Criminal Justice System: Standards Probation*, Edinburgh, Scottish Executive.

Scottish Executive (2004g) *National Objectives for Social Work Services in the Criminal Justice System: Standards Community Service*, Edinburgh, Scottish Executive.

Scottish Executive (2004h) 'Antisocial behaviour measures come into force' [online], press release, http://www.scotland.gov.uk/News/Releases/2004/10/28095758 (Accessed 19 January 2007).

Scottish Executive (2004i) *Police Restorative Warnings in Scotland: Guidelines for the Police*, Edinburgh, Scottish Executive.

Scottish Executive (2005) *National Standards for Victims of Crime*, Edinburgh, Scottish Executive.

Scottish Executive (2006a) 'Criminal proceedings in the Scottish courts 2004/5', *Statistical Bulletin*, CrJ/2006/3, Edinburgh, Scottish Executive.

Scottish Executive (2006b) *Reducing Reoffending: National Strategy for the Management of Offenders*, Edinburgh, Scottish Executive.

Scottish Executive (2006c) 'Criminal justice social work statistics, 2004–5', *Statistical Bulletin*, CrJ/2006/01, Edinburgh, Scottish Executive.

Scottish Executive (2006d) *Getting it Right for Every Child: Implementation Plan*, Edinburgh, Scottish Executive.

Scottish Executive (2006e) *Use of Antisocial Behaviour Orders in Scotland: Report of the 2005/6 Survey*, Scottish Executive Social Research, Edinburgh, Scottish Executive.

Scottish Law Commission (2002) *Report on Age of Criminal Responsibility*, Scot Law Com. no.185, Edinburgh, The Stationery Office.

Scottish Office (1999) *Health, Social Work and Related Services for Mentally Disordered Offenders in Scotland*, Edinburgh, The Stationery Office.

Scottish Office and Health Department (1998) *Interviewing People who are Mentally Disordered*, Edinburgh, HMSO.

Scottish Parliament Information Centre (SPICe) (1999) *Mentally Disordered Offenders in Scotland*, Edinburgh, Scottish Parliament.

Scottish Social Services Council (SSSC) (2002) *Code of Practice for Social Care Workers*, Dundee, SSSC.

Sentencing Commission for Scotland (2006a) *The Scope to Improve Consistency in Sentencing Report*, Edinburgh, Sentencing Commission for Scotland.

Sentencing Commission for Scotland (2006b) *Early Release from Prison and Supervision of Prisoners on their Release*, Edinburgh, Sentencing Commission for Scotland.

Singleton, N., Meltzer, H. and Gatward, R. (1998) *Psychiatric Morbidity Among Prisoners in England and Wales*, Office for National Statistics, London, The Stationery Office

Smith, D. (2002) 'Social work with offenders' in Adams, R., Dominelli, L. and Payne, M. (eds) *Social Work: Themes, Issues and Critical Debates* (2nd edn), Basingstoke, Palgrave.

Smith, M. and Milligan, I. (2004) 'The expansion of secure accommodation in Scotland: in the best interests of the child?', *Youth Justice*, vol. 4, no. 3, p. 178.

Social Work Services and Prison Inspectorate for Scotland (1998) *Women Offenders – A Safer Way*, Edinburgh, The Stationery Office.

Social Work Services Group (1991) *National Objectives and Standards for Social Work Services in the Criminal Justice System*, Edinburgh, Scottish Office.

Social Work Services Inspectorate (SWSI) (1996) *Helping the Court Decide: Report of an Inspection of Social Enquiry Reports for the Criminal Courts*, Edinburgh, SWSI.

Social Work Services Inspectorate (SWSI) (1997) *A Commitment to Protect*, Edinburgh, Scottish Office.

Social Work Services Inspectorate (SWSI) (2000) *Management and Assessment of Risk in Social Work Services*, Edinburgh, Scottish Office/SWSI.

Summary Justice Review Committee (2004) *The Summary Justice Review Committee: Report to Ministers*, Edinburgh, Scottish Executive (McInnes Report).

Walker, M., Barclay, A., Hunter, L., Kendrick, A., Malloch, M., Hill, M. and McIvor, G. (2006) 'Secure accommodation in Scotland: its role and relationship with "alternative" services', *Social Research*, Edinburgh, Scottish Executive.

Whyte, B. (1998) 'Rediscovering juvenile delinquency' in Lockyer, A. and Stone, F. (eds) *Juvenile Justice in Scotland*, Edinburgh, T. and T. Clark.

Whyte, B. (2001) *Criminal Justice Social Work in Scotland: Policy and Practice*, Edinburgh, Criminal Justice Social Work Development Centre for Scotland.

Whyte, B. (2004) 'Young and persistent: Recent developments in youth justice policy and practice in Scotland', *Youth Justice*, vol. 3, no. 2, p. 74.

Whyte, B. (2005) *What Works with Children and Young People Involved in Crime?*, Edinburgh, Criminal Justice Social Work Development Centre for Scotland.

Young, P. (1997) *Crime and Criminal Justice in Scotland*, Edinburgh, The Stationery Office.

Youth Justice Improvement Group (2006) *Report of the Youth Justice Improvement Group: Proposals for Action*, Edinburgh, Scottish Executive.

Zedner, L. (2004) *Criminal Justice*, Oxford, Oxford University Press.

# Acknowledgements

Grateful acknowledgement is made to the following sources for permission to reproduce material within this product.

## Figures

*Figure 1*: 'Criminal proceedings in the Scottish courts 2004/5", *Statistical Bulletin*, Criminal Justice Series, CrJ/2006/3, The Scottish Executive; *Figure 2*: McNeill, F., Batchelor, S. Burnett, R. and Knox, J. (2005) *21st Century Social Work Review: Reducing Reoffending: Key Practice Skills*, The Scottish Executive; *Figure 3*: *Supporting Safer, Stronger Communities: Scotland's Criminal Justice Plan* (2004) The Scottish Executive; *Figure 9*: 'Criminal proceedings in the Scottish courts 2004/5", *Statistical Bulletin*, Criminal Justice Series, CrJ/2006/3, The Scottish Executive; *Figure 10*: DTZ Pieda Consulting (2005) *Measurement of the Extent of Youth Crime in Scotland*, The Scottish Executive; *Figure 11*: *Dealing with Offending by Young People Summary Report* (2002) Audit Scotland; *Figure 13*: Laing, J. (1999) *Care or Custody?: Mentally Disordered Offenders in the Criminal Justice System*, Oxford University Press.

## Illustrations

*Cover*: © Dynamic Graphics Group/IT Stock Free/Alamy; *pages 31, 38, 63, and 97*: www.johnbirdsall.co.uk.